A Review of [

Barbara Harris Whitfield's post-operative near-death experience (NDE) in 1975 transformed her from a materially-oriented housewife and mother into a spiritual crusader.

She went back to college to become a healthcare professional, studied NDE aftereffects with me in the 1980s, became the first woman elected to the IANDS Board of Directors, co-founded one of the longest-running Friends of IANDS support groups, embraced the "child within" model of spiritual development and applied it to NDErs, taught college courses in psychospiritual recovery from trauma and addiction, and published four previous books and a host of articles on spiritual growth.

The Natural Soul, her most recent offering, pulls together her life's work into an insightful and practical guide to living from our soul rather from our ego. This book is not about an instantaneous spiritual transformation that occurred when Whitfield awoke from her NDE 35 years ago. It is rather about a gradual accumulation of insights, a spiritual journey that was initiated, in her case, by the NDE, but which evolved over decades. (review continued on next page)

Bruce Greyson, M.D., is the Chester F. Carlson Professor of Psychiatry and Neurobehavioral Sciences and Director of the Division of Perceptual Studies at the University of Virginia School of Medicine

Past President and Director of Research for The International Association for Near-Death Studies

[1] This review first appeared in the winter 2010 issue of the Journal of Near-Death Studies, Volume 28, number 2. Copyright ©2010: International Association of Near-Death Studies. Reprinted with permission. See: www.iands.org

Whitfield used NDEs to illustrate what it means to live from the soul rather than from the ego. For example, the life review in NDEs is often described as if it were a reminiscence in anticipation of dying, a psychological summing up of the value of one's life (Butler, 1963; Noyes & Kletti, 1977). It is those things, but Ian Stevenson and Emily Cook (1995) concluded from a systematic review of NDEs with life reviews that they have deeper implications and that they make sense only in the context a life beyond this material one. Whitfield in The Natural Soul explored that context in depth. She revealed the life review as not just a recall of memories but a first-hand experience of oneness with others, as the experiencer relives the events not only from one's own perspective but also through the eyes of others involved:

•••

"In every scene of my life review I could feel again what I had felt. . . and I could feel everything that everyone else had felt as a consequence of my presence and my actions. Some of it felt good and some of it felt awful. . . .

The information came in, and then love neutralized my judgments against myself. No matter how I judged myself in each interaction, being held by God was the bigger interaction. God interjected love into everything. . . .

This was when I first realized that we do not end at our skin. We are all in this big churning mass of consciousness." (pp. 5-8)

•••

In this sense, the life review is far more than just a reassessment of life events. It is a lived encounter with the fact that we humans are all one, which puts the death of the individual in a very different light. Indeed, Whitfield showed how the life review can be a means of seeking (or creating) meaning in the problems and conflicts of life. In the Foreword to this book, her husband Charles Whitfield noted that this act of "making meaning from our everyday experiences and conflicts" is an important part of soul work that enables us "to rise above the limited and often painful episodes of our life" (p. ix).

But although Whitfield made good use of NDEs as an exemplar of spiritual interactions, her message extends far beyond NDEs – in fact, far beyond mystical experiences in general – to encompass how we negotiate our daily lives. So much has been written and

(continued on page 149)

Endorsements

When people have a Near-Death Experience, they transition from a body-based to a soul-based consciousness, and in that soul-state is granted for a moment outside of time a kind of all-knowing understanding. Now suppose you could hold that state of consciousness so that you could distill and communicate that knowledge to others. Well, this is precisely what Barbara Whitfield has done in her remarkable newbook, *The Natural Soul*, which does indeed provide a feast of soul-food for the mind.

Kenneth Ring, Ph.D.,
Emeritus Professor of Psychology, University of Connecticut Author of *Lessons from the Light*

In *The Natural Soul* Barbara Whitfield takes us on a journey to our Essence, our True Selves. She shows us, in a deeply meaningful way, the Creator Selves that we are. Through intimate and meaningful personal revelation she makes real the teachings of the mystical masters and the core beliefs of essential religion. This is a remarkable book which makes "intimately real" our true journey through birth and death onto our continual Essence.

Maurie D.Pressman, M.D.,
Emeritus Chairman of Psychiatry, Albert Einstein Medical Center, Philadelphia Emeritus Clinical Professor of Psychiatry, Temple University School of Medicine Author of *Visions From the Soul: Enter the Supermind*

Whitfield shows us what is missing for optimum health and peace of mind. Going beyond the conventional medical model of prescription pills for every ailment, she describes how we can nurture our health through the innate power within our natural Soul.

Alan Gaby, M.D.,
Past president,American Holistic Medical Association Author of *Preventing and Reversing Osteoporosis*

The Natural Soul gently and powerfully guides readers to reconnect with their core Self — their true essence, their Soul. For spiritual seekers, this book affirms the path they travel, and provides skills and hope around what it means to be fully human. Barbara Whitfield writes this book from her heart. It will open the hearts of those who read it as well. The Natural Soul is an exceptional contribution for our challenging times.

Judith S. Miller Ph.D.,
Professor of Human Development, Columbia University
Author of *Direct Connection: Transformation of Consciousness*

This book has a big theme that illustrates that the more we live from our authentic Soul — the more our Soul and the Souls of our loved ones expand. And this may be part of the Divine Mystery of what life here is really all about. Whitfield shows us how the deeply meaningful experiences in life including our relationships with our children and grandchildren will help them to remember that they were Spirit before they were born and will be Spirit again after this lifetime. An excellent read.

Sandra Sedgbeer, editor Children of the New Earth
Magazine, Inspired Parenting Magazine,
Planetlightworker.com Magazine

A lovely and sensitive book, which will be very comforting to those who have suffered a major loss, and enlightening to those who haven't.

Jennifer Schneider, M.D.,
Author of *Living with Chronic Pain* and *Back From Betrayal*

Skillfully touches on the pivotal stages of life, from birth to death, and much in between. With an emphasis on experiencing life from the perspective of our Soul, Barbara Whitfield brings love, comfort, soothing, and ease to each and every milestone one might encounter. A comforting and peaceful book, it makes a great read for challenging times.

Karen Bishop,
Author of *The Ascension Primer: Life in the Higher Realms*

The Natural Soul is a beautifully woven tapestry of the author's deep wisdom, spiritual experiences, and personal stories, revealing how a near-death experience affects all important aspects of a person's life. By the end of the book, the reader is not only wiser, but feels a connection and friendship with the genuine "Natural Soul."

> Yolaine Stout, President and Executive Director, American Center for the Integration of Spiritually Transformative Experiences

The soul is limitless Life and Love Being, and the stories shared in *The Natural Soul* left me with a profound understanding of this truth. Barbara writes that our Soul is who we are right now - not some kind of Spiritual concept or higher part of us 'out there'. It is who we really are if we only take a moment to look at and feel our real self. It is who we are before life, during life,and after life. Indeed,our soul is life itself; eternal, unbreakable, and in every moment connected to all those we love regardless of distance or on which side of the veil we or they reside.

> Dana Mrkich, Author of A New Chapter, Sydney, Australia

A work of art that helps us shift from a fear based sense of death too one that embraces its nature and opens the door of its Mystery. Barbara's compelling words weave a story of inspiration where the reader will find hope. It invites the Soul to soar.

> Jyoti (Jeneane Prevatt,PhD), Author of *An Angel Called My Name*, and co-author of *The Power of Humility* Russell Park, PhD., Clinical Psychologist, Co-author of *The Power of Humility*

Your recovery story is amazing and I appreciate how you have remained focused on bringing great detail and guidance for those on the path of light and True Self.

> Omer G.

As Above, So Below

Nebula: *n.* pl. neb·u·lae or neb·u·las. 1. Astronomy. a. A diffuse mass of interstellar dust or gas or both, visible as luminous patches or areas of darkness.

On the cover is an authentic photograph of the Helix Nebula, actually a composite of images taken by NASA's Hubble Space Telescope and at the Kitt Peak National Observatory in Arizona. It was featured on NASA's website as an Astronomy Picture of the Day in May 2003 and thereafter reproduced on a number of websites under the title "The Eye of God".

This nebula has been described by astronomers as "a trillion-mile-long tunnel of glowing gases" and it lies about 700 light-years away. It's width is about 2.5 light-years.

It shows what is called a "Light Echo." The light from an exploded star is bouncing off of space dust in the same way as a yodeler's voice echoes off of mountains. Eventually the light reaches earth. Perhaps, and I believe, that love from our Soul works the same way. Our Soul's love echoes and bounces off of each other's Souls already and always.

Barbara

The Natural Soul

Unity with the Spiritual Energy
that connects us to our self,
others and God

*What It looks like and
how It feels*

Barbara Harris Whitfield

ꟽꞪP
muse house press

The Natural Soul

Unity with the Spiritual Energy
that connects us to our self,
others and God

*What It looks like and
how It feels*

Barbara Harris Whitfield

ᛗᚻP
muse house press

MHP
muse house press
PENNINGTON PUBLISHERS

ISBN 978-0-615-33003-7

First Trade Paperback edition: January 2010
© Copyright 2009 Barbara Harris Whitfield
All Rights reserved

Request for information and rights should be addressed to:
Muse House Press

Find us on the Internet at:

www.PenningtonPublishers.com
www.MuseHousePress.com
www.BarbaraWhitfield.com

Muse House Press and the MHP logo are imprints of Pennington Publishers,Inc.

Cover design: Donald Brennan / YakRider Media
Interior design: Donald Brennan / YakRider Media

Up to 10% of each chapter may be reproduced as quotes provided attribution to the author is made. Other use may only be made with prior written permission of the publisher.

Printed in the United States of America

Acknowledgements

This book began because of the inspiration of Steve Rother. He then connected me with Sandie Sedgbeer; who helped me develop its form and edit it. These two were instrumental in the writing of this book.

My husband, Charles Whitfield, was there with patience and the ability to keep me expanding my explanations. His suggestions and writing skills are reflected though out this book.

Our four kids are a joy to walk through this life with. Beth, Steve and Gary keep us in our Soul, as does Kate, who is a major contributor to this writing. I hope some day she is writing the acknowledgement page for her own published book. She has a big Soul and a lot to say.

Our four kids have expanded to 19. We have four in-law children now. Ed Graves, Andrew Hart, Robin Harris and recently Annie Harris was added to our "gang" in a beautiful garden wedding where she and Gary exchanged vows by the Chattahoochee River.

My daughter Beth Sheryl Graves has taught me much about compassion and also about healthy boundaries. Much of what I write about Soul parenting and also about allowing children to naturally grieve and express all their feelings-- I learned from her. I'd like to say she learned it from me and maybe she did but... Beth has given me my greatest pleasure as I have watched her grow into motherhood.

Watching her as a mom with our grandson Ethan warms my heart in the way parents hope for as they watch their own kids grow into parenting. And, I also need to thank Robin and Annie for the great relationship we have. I love their company and everything else they share with me.

I need to thank Steve and Gary Harris, Andrew Hart and Ed Graves for being the best fathers to watch in action. They give me hope for future generations because until now I haven't seen what good fathering looks like. They engage our grandchildren in the way kids deserve to be treated.

Our grandchildren — Jacob, Nicholas, Joey, Ethan, Thomas, Anna, Jonathan, Alexander and Lily — add joy to our life all the time.

I want to acknowledge all the kind Souls who contributed to this book: Ken Ring, Bruce Greyson, Dennis Brooks, Jyoti, Russell Park, Karen Bishop, Omer Gillham, Chris Norman, Sharon Cormier, Laurie Anderson Peters, Susan Allison, Rick Bach, Beth Pullen, Robynne Moran, Francesca Sorentino, Michael Sorentino, Betsy Stevenson, Chuck Darlington, Paul Furgalack, Chris and Jen Lyons, Theresa Rose, Emma Rose, Lynda Cummings, Carol Madec Scoville, Kim Wise, Marshall and Eunice Silverman, Emil and Eileen Krupkin, Julius and Florence Silverman, Ira and Bernice Wagman, Cookie Frankel, Leonard Bassin and Tom Sawyer.

And finally, a grateful thanks to Donald Brennan for his technological expertise and his expansive creativity.

Dedication

To Noah Lyons
A courageous Soul
Who came here
For one brief instant
To touch all of us.
Thank you, Noah, for your gift.

Table of Contents

Foreword

by

Charles L. Whitfield, M.D.

This is a remarkable book. Reading it nourishes our Soul (Essence or Real Self). It creatively defines and describes our Soul in a number of ways, including by giving many examples of what its author Barbara Whitfield has learned from her and others' ordinary and sometimes extraordinary life experiences.

From Socrates and Plato to Carl Jung, the notion of the Soul pervades many disciplines and has done so over the last 3 millennia. We read and hear so much *about* the Soul. In this writing, we are being shown the Soul. We are being shown how it works when we get our ego out of the way and let the Soul live and express in its natural state. And, we do this by letting go of our past wounds, or what Barbara calls "toxic pain," and then letting go of our need to control so our Soul can orchestrate our lives. This book takes you step by step through this process. And it helps you to go through this process with your loved ones through life's ups and downs, through bringing Souls into this world and again at the end of this life, helping our loved ones leave.

What is the Soul?

Here are some simple definitions from people on the street.

- Your Soul is your existence.

- It's who you are. Your body is one thing. Your Soul is another.

- When you die, you're identified by your Soul.

- It's the Spirit of God.

- It lives for eternity.

- It is the image of God in man.

- Your true inner self, your true being.

Barbara Whitfield was a researcher for 6 years at University of Connecticut School of Medicine and has written and lectured widely on Spirituality and Near-Death Experiences. In this book, she explains evidence for the Soul's existence before birth and even after the physical body dies. Just as important, she shows us how to live as our Soul and relate to the Souls of others.

Science and the Soul

While science has not established the existence of the human Soul, that doesn't mean there isn't one, since science does not yet have the means to identify and measure a Soul. As scientist and Spiritual writer Ken Wilber has observed, the existence of the Soul and Spirit cannot be proven by the scientific method. Indeed, the scientific method can usually only accurately address the physical realm of our existence. To address the mind, we have to move above and beyond the scientific method alone and use observation (phenomenology) and interpretation (hermeneutics). But to address the Soul we have to go beyond these three methods alone and use ontology, which is the study of being, existence, and experience. A principle way to measure these include our shared experience, whether spoken, written or expressed graphically through art. In this book, Barbara Whitfield presents numerous such shared experiences that add to our collective documentation of the existence of the Soul.

Gifts of the Soul

Barbara expands our view of reality to show us there are more important things in life than being a consumer or what the media tries to tell and sell us. And in this expansion lies our hope that she is carefully laying out in this book. Living a life with this constructive and enlivening attitude that comes so easily from our Soul, we find peace and joy because, as she explains and we have observed, peace and joy are the natural state of our existence when we live from our Soul.

An important part of Soul work and Spirituality is making meaning from our everyday experiences and conflicts. When we make meaning this way we are able to rise above the limited and often painful episodes in our life. This book gives us several useful examples of such making meaning, including the creative process of reframing. For example, on page 87 in the chapter on grieving, she addresses depression and reframes it as *stuck grief.* In this way there is both movement and meaning. If we believe we are "depressed" there is no movement or resolution. Then society gives us a pill to numb us, which often only distracts us and commonly deepens our stuck grief. In the reframe, we can realize that our stuck grief can be lived and worked through. She takes us step by step through the grieving process, showing us how this healing movement works. She shows us how to eliminate our suffering by embracing and metabolizing our pain. We learn experientially that suffering comes from resisting our pain. When we let go and allow our pain to come up, we understand how bittersweet grieving is because we get relief.

If our grief work is because we have lost a loved one, Barbara gives us even more of a positive outcome than we have known before. She explains how whoever departs, leaves us with a bigger Soul because we take in and keep all of our love from them and for them. This may even give us an experiential understanding of a quote that many have never understood by *Kahlil Gibran.* He said "Your joy is your sorrow unmasked."

I believe that our ego could never understand what Gibran wrote, but our Soul knows it. When we let go and relax into our grief work, we peel off the layers until all that is left is our natural Soul's joy.

The Natural Soul will open your heart and show you the way.

Charles L. Whitfield, M.D.
Author of the bestselling *Healing the Child Within*
Atlanta, Georgia
April, 2009

"The near-death experience, and particularly the life review, is often described as a summing up of the events of one's life. *The Natural Soul* reveals that it is far more than that. It is also a first-hand experience of oneness with others, of the fact that we are not separate, which puts the death (and indeed the life) of the individual in a very different light. Barbara Whitfield shows that what near-death experiencers (and in fact all of us) long for is not another dimension, but rather who we are in that dimension — and she shows us how to experience ourselves as those Souls right here, right now. It is a paradox that we go to great lengths to find the source of happiness, which Whitfield shows us is already and always the natural state of the Soul. Both religious tradition and contemporary science seem to miss this basic point, as they struggle to help us 'understand' what would come naturally if we only lived as Souls rather than as egos. Whitfield shows us not how to 'understand' reality but how to live it."

Bruce Greyson, M.D.,
Chester F. Carlson Professor of Psychiatry
& Neurobehavioral Sciences.
Director of the Division of Perceptual Studies
at the University of Virginia.

Introduction

My work with dying people probably would have never come about if I hadn't died myself. I know that sounds strange. How many of us die and get to come back and talk about it? Not many, we may think, but that's not true. In 1981, a Gallup poll reported that one in every nineteen Americans has had a Near-Death Experience (NDE). And these first numbers included only adults. Since that time we have acquired data on childhood NDEs, which reveals that they are almost as prevalent as adult experiences.

I want to share my own NDE with you, most importantly to tell you about what we call the "life review." Our research shows that only in about twenty-three percent of NDEs is there a life review.[1] The life review is a panoramic playback of virtually everything that has ever happened in one's life. Since my NDE 33 years ago, I have focused my heart and my life on the knowledge I received from my life review. For six years in the 1980s I worked as a researcher at the University of Connecticut Medical School, interviewing people who have had Near-Death Experiences. When I write or speak about mine, I draw on these six years of research so that my own story also reflects the experiences that my colleagues and I have heard about and studied.

The Life Review as the Ultimate Teaching Tool

Some people who have experienced a life review report seeing their life as if they are watching the pages in a book. Others describe it as a film. My life review appeared as a cloud filled with thousands of bubbles. In each bubble there was a scene from my life. I had the feeling I could bob from bubble to bubble, but overall the experience felt like a linear sequence in which I relived all thirty-two years of my life. This felt totally *experiential*. The knowledge I was given was derived from direct experience (as opposed to other methods of acquired learning).

During a life review, many of us don't just experience our own feelings; but we also experience the feelings of everyone else, as though all

---

[1] Bruce Greyson, MD, Director of Research for the International Association for Near-Death Studies (IANDS), personal communication.

other people participating in our lifetimes are joined. This gives us an immediate and powerful understanding of the effect that all our words, actions and behaviors have had on those around us. We come to understand that we don't end at our skin. It is an illusion that we are separate. This deep review of our life effectively demonstrates that, at a higher level of consciousness, we are all connected. We could say that our Souls are connected.

This new perspective totally changes our values and attitudes about the way we want to live. Materialism decreases for us and altruistic values become greater in most Near-Death Experiencers' (NDErs) lives. Almost all of us talk about a sense of mission. If we were Spiritual before, the shift in values and attitude is not as apparent as it is in someone like me who had become an atheist when I numbed out (from child abuse and neglect) at an early age. Later, after my NDE with its powerful Life Review, my changes have been obvious and profound. An important change for me was switching from *believing* I was an atheist for decades, to this sudden *knowing* of who I really was: a *Soul* connected to my *Higher Self* and my *Higher Power*. (See map of these three crucial parts of us that become one, which we call "The *Sacred Person*" on page 33). Another important change for myself and many of the Near-Death Experiencers I interviewed was a need to live an authentic life as a crucial part of this threesome or *Sacred Person*. I needed to live and relate from my Soul to the Souls of others.

This is not an easy task in our "modern" world. The media tells us our happiness comes from shopping and we will find peace and happiness if we consume. If our lives are filled with the noise of our culture — politics, advertising, consumerism, threats of terrorism, and the like — we get lost in the stress of it all. We lose our connection to our authentic self — our Soul. This book is an attempt to explain how my life and the lives of my loved ones and friends have evolved to give us the experience of living from our Souls — a heart-felt life that has slowed down and become peaceful because we live from this natural state.

My Near-Death Experiences started this search 33 years ago, so please remember this did not happen over night. But the journey has been worth it, as you will read.

Our Natural State

When we are living from our Soul, our True Self, and we invite our Higher Self into our conscious physical being, it brings with it that which we have craved our entire life. At our core we are Spirit and we discover our root Spiritual feelings: peace and joy. When we lived from our ego, peace and joy were enigmas that had something to do with sex[2], drugs or "power." They were feelings that were either beyond us or got us into trouble. Now that we live from and as our Soul, we are beginning to realize that we *naturally are Spirit, and peace and joy are our Soul's natural feeling state when we get our ego out of our own way and let Spirit enliven us.*

This quote from *A Course in Miracles* poetically describes our memory of our natural state of being:

> "Listen, — perhaps you catch a hint of an ancient state not quite forgotten; dim, perhaps, and yet not altogether unfamiliar, like a song whose name is long forgotten, and the circumstances in which you heard completely unremembered. Not the whole song has stayed with you, but just a little wisp of melody, attached not to a person or a place or anything particular. But you remember, from just this little part, how lovely was the song..." *(ACIM 446t, 6:1-3).*

In each chapter of this book I will explain a part of our life experience that can help us magnify our Soul at its richest and fullest, as well as the Soul of our loved ones so we may more easily join in this sacred dance of life.

Not all experiences are joyful. Our life has its ups and downs, and we have painful experiences. But we can embrace the painful and the joyful in a Soulful way so that each milestone strengthens our Soul's connection to our self and our loved ones. We can realize experientially over time that, although there are still painful losses in life, these can be experienced as pain — not suffering — if we are living our lives as our Soul.

---

[2] The reference above is about sex as an addiction or habituation. For those of us who are living as our Soul/True Self sex becomes a sacrament. For more on Spiritual sex, see Whitfield B (1995) Spiritual Awakenings.

Just as an acorn contains the potential for its identity, a giant oak tree, we, too, contain the potential at birth for our Soul to develop to its fullest in this lifetime.

—Barbara Harris Whitfield

It's early in the morning on a weekday. Lily is beaming at me, behind the camera. We are daycare four days-a-week.

This little bundle of joy is like the acorn and Charlie represents the oak. However, as you will read in the second chapter, she is also our *teacher*.

Chapter I

My Life Review

My last book, *The Power of Humility*, was co-authored with Charles Whitfield, Jyoti and Russell Park. The book is really a map of transcendence. It shows us how to use our relationships as our Spiritual path. The entire book can be summed up by the simple map below.

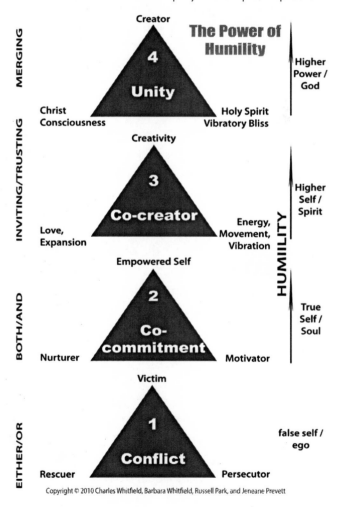

Copyright © 2010 Charles Whitfield, Barbara Whitfield, Russell Park, and Jeneane Prevett

We start with **Level 1, Conflict**, which is where humans have been bumping around forever. This map then points us up to **Level 2,** where we realize we have choices. We don't have to accept painful and often disabling conflict in relationships anymore. By using the power of humility in this way, we transcend *either/or* thinking and move up to *both/and* thinking which allows for infinite choices so that our relationships can be dedicated to **co-commitment**. Then the *empowered self* of **Level 2** is transformed into a **co-creative** *energy* and *action*, which is **Level 3**. At this level of development, it's as if we become partners with God. We sense the flow and perfection of God in our life, we act in ways that creatively manifest our now expanded intent, and we love unconditionally while we do it.

Level 4 includes and expands our awareness of what we call our *Sacred Person: True Self, Higher Self* and *Higher Power* or *God.* When we are totally alive and no longer need to spend any energy living from an ego or false self, living as our Sacred Person is Level 4. When we ask for help at this level, it comes almost immediately in ways we couldn't have predicted. This help comes with integrity and tenderness. We are flooded with knowledge about ourselves, the other person or the relationship. It appears like a Life Review. We feel what the other person is feeling. We see the bigger picture. And we trust God's Divine Energy to work in others as it is working in us.

Example of Levels 3 and 4

In my Near-Death Experience (NDE) I was given a life review. I relived all 32 years of my life. In earth time it took 20 minutes, but I experienced it as though it was all happening again just as it had the first time. This experience happened to me in 1975 but I remember it as though it happened a few hours ago. It is always with me and I try to live my life according to what I realized as God held me during it. We together as my Sacred Person experienced my life again through God's eyes.

When Jyoti and Russ presented the one-page map to us, I kept staring at the two higher levels. I knew I knew them. I was trying to live my life there. I had been trying for years and it was possible: I had glimpses, even interludes. But I had given up trying to explain it. Suddenly, as I stared at the map, I realized that this was the opportunity to explain what I knew in my heart for so many years but couldn't articulate.

We worked on *The Power of Humility* for five years. It was slow; sometimes we had to put it away for awhile, and sometimes insights came in bursts that gave us renewed enthusiasm. While we were slowly going through the material, I was writing this book too. I was pouring my heart into my computer because the examples I tell illustrate what we were working carefully to explain in a comprehensive conceptual framework in *The Power of Humility*.

My Near-Death Experience

I was born with a deformity, a curvature in my lumbar spine called "scoliosis." It never bothered me until 1973 when it suddenly became the focus of my life. I was hospitalized four times in the next two years, each time for two weeks, with traction and injections of Demerol to help alleviate the pain. Looking back on it now, I believe, like many other NDErs, that my back pain was a metaphor for my life, which had gotten off track.

Finally, I underwent surgery, a spinal fusion. I awoke after the five-and-a-half-hour operation in a Stryker-frame circle bed. This strange bed looks like a Ferris wheel for one person. There are two big chrome hoops with a stretcher suspended in the middle. I remained in that bed for almost a month, and then I was placed in a full body cast from my armpits to my knees for six months.

About two days after surgery, complications set in and I started to die. I remember waking up in the circle bed and seeing this huge belly. I had swollen up, and the swelling was pulling my incisions open and it hurt. I called for my nurse, and then I started screaming.

People in white came rushing in. It was a dramatic scene, just like those you see in hospital dramas on television. I had no idea what was going on because I hadn't become a respiratory therapist yet. It seemed like everybody was pushing carts and machinery, throwing things back and forth over me. They hooked me up to all kinds of machinery, tubes, monitors and bags. Overwhelmed emotionally, I lost consciousness and later that night woke up in the hall outside my room. I floated back into the room and saw my body. I felt peaceful, more peaceful than I had ever been in this lifetime. Then I went into a tunnel where I was greeted and held by my grandmother who had been dead for 14 years. Before this I had never once thought about her surviving her death. I didn't believe in that. But now I knew I was with her. Her love enveloped me and together we relived all our memories of each other. I could see and feel all this through her eyes and her feelings of each moment too. And I know she experienced how her actions and her love had comforted me in my childhood.

Suddenly I was back in my body, back in the circle bed. Two nurses were opening my drapes. The sunlight was startling. It hurt my eyes. I asked them to close the drapes. I tried to tell my nurses and then several doctors that I had left the bed. They told me that it was impossible and that I had been hallucinating.

My Life Review

About a week later, I again left my body in the circle bed. I was no longer on the critical list, but I was still debilitated and weak. I had been rotated forward onto my face. I was uncomfortable. I seemed to have been in that position for too long. I reached for the call button, but it had slipped away from where it had been clipped to the bed sheet. I started to call, then yell, then scream frantically, but my door was closed. No one came. I became hysterical. I separated from my body.

As I left my body, I again went out into the darkness, only this time I was awake and could see it happening. Looking down and off to the right, I saw myself in a bubble — in the circle bed — crying. Then I looked up and to the left, and I saw my one-year-old self in another bubble-face down in my crib — crying just as hard. I looked to the right and saw myself again in the circle bed, then to the left and saw myself as a baby. I looked back and forth about three more times, then I let go. I decided I did not want to be the thirty-two-year-old Barbara anymore; I'd go to the baby. As I moved away from my body in the circle bed, I felt as though I released myself from this lifetime. As I did, I became aware of an Energy that was wrapping itself around me and going through me, permeating me, holding up every molecule of my being.

Even though I had been an atheist for years, I felt God's love. This love was holding me. It felt incredible. There are no words in the English language, or maybe in this reality, to explain the kind of love God emanates. God was *totally accepting* of everything we — God and I — reviewed in my life.

In every scene of my life review I could feel again what I had felt at various times in my life. And I could feel *everything* that everyone else had felt as a consequence of my presence and my actions. Some of it felt good and some of it felt awful. All of this translated into knowledge, *and I learned. Oh, how I learned!*

The information was flowing at an incredible speed that probably would have burned me up if it hadn't been for the extraordinary Energy holding me. The information came in, and then love neutralized my judgments against myself. In other words, throughout every scene I viewed, information flowed through me about my perceptions and feelings, and the perceptions and feelings of every person who had shared those scenes with me. No matter how I judged myself in each interaction, being held by God was the bigger interaction. God interjected love into everything, every feeling, every bit of information about absolutely everything that went on, so that everything was all right. There was no good and no bad. There was only me — and my loved ones from this life — trying to survive... just trying to *be*.

I realize now that without God holding me, I would not have had the strength to experience what I did.

When it started, God and I were merging. We became one, so that I could see through God's eyes and feel through God's heart. Together, we witnessed how severely I had treated myself because that was the behavior shown and taught to me as a child. I realized that the only big mistake I had made in my thirty-two years of life was that I had never learned to love myself.

God let me into God's experience of all this. I felt God's memories of these scenes through God's eyes. I could sense God's divine intelligence, and it was astonishing. God loves us and wants us to wake up to our real selves, to what is important. I realized that *God wants us to know that we only experience real pain if we die without living first.* And the way to live is to give love to ourselves and to others. It seems that we are here to learn to give and receive love. But only when we heal enough to be real can we understand and give and receive love the way love was meant to be.

When God holds us in our life reviews and we merge into One, we remember this feeling as being limitless. God is limitless. God's capacity to love is never-ending. God's love for us never changes, no matter how we are. God doesn't judge us either. During our life review, we judge ourselves by *feeling* the love we have created in other's lives. We also feel the pain we have caused in other's lives. This may be a kind of Cosmic Equalizer.

I did not see an old man with a white beard who sits in judgment of us. I only felt limitless divine love.

God only gives. God interjected love into all the scenes of my life to show me God's reality. And the most amazing part of all is that God held nothing back. I understood all that God understood. God let me in. God shared all of God's self with me: all the qualities of gentleness and openness, and all the gifts, including our own empowerment and peace. I never knew that much loving intelligence and freedom could exist.

What I saw in My Life Review

At this point God and I were merging into one Sacred Person. It felt as though I lifted off the circle bed and We went to the baby I was seeing to my upper left in the darkness. Picture the baby being in a bubble; that bubble was in the center of a cloud of thousands and thousands of bubbles. In each bubble was another scene from my life. As we moved toward the baby, it was as though we were bobbing through the bubbles. At the same time, there was a linear sequence in which we relived thirty-two years of my life. I could hear myself saying, "No wonder, no wonder." I now believe my "no wonders" meant "No wonder you are the way you are now. Look what was done to you when you were a little girl."

My mother had been dependent on prescription drugs, angry and abusive, and my father wasn't home much of the time and did little to intervene. I saw all this again, but I did not see it in little bits and pieces, the way I had remembered it as an adult. I saw and experienced it just as I had lived it at the time it first happened. Not only was I me, I was also my mother, my dad, and my brother. We were all one. Just as I had felt everything my grandmother had felt, I now felt my mother's pain and neglect from her childhood. She wasn't trying to be mean. She didn't know how to be loving or kind. She didn't know how to love. She didn't understand what life is really all about. And she was still angry from her own childhood, angry because they were poor and because her father was sick almost every day until he died when she was eleven. And then she was angry because he had left her. She didn't know what to do with her anger so she gave it to my brother and me. Her anger boiled up all the time and then she physically abused us or she made us listen to all her resentments. Her list went back to her early childhood. Everyone had hurt her. I don't think that she, through her numbness and drugged state, understood how she was doing the same thing to us.

Everything came flooding back, including my father's helplessness and confusion at stopping the insanity. I could hear myself saying, "No wonder, no wonder." And then the benevolent Energy that was holding me held me tighter and with even more love.

We continued watching my mother in pain, always seeing doctors and always receiving prescription pain killers, sleeping pills and tranquilizers. My only feeling during this time was loneliness. I saw myself down on my knees by the side of my bed, praying for a doctor to help my mother. I saw how I had given up "myself" in order to survive. I forgot that I was a child. I became my mother's mother. I suddenly knew that my mother had had the same thing happen to her in her childhood. She took care of her father, and as a child she gave herself up to take care of him. As children, she and I both became anything and everything others needed. As my life review continued, I also saw my mother's Soul, how painful her life was, how lost she was. And I saw my father, and how he put blinders on himself to avoid his grief over my mother's pain and to survive. In my life review, I saw that they were good people caught in helplessness. I saw their beauty, their humanity and their needs that had gone unattended to in their own childhoods. I loved them and understood them. We may have been trapped, but we were still Souls connected in our dance of life by an Energy source that had created us.

This was when I first realized that we do not end at our skin. We are all in this big churning mass of consciousness. We are each a part of this consciousness we call God. And we are not just human. We are Spirit. We were Spirit before we came into this lifetime. We are all struggling Spirits now, trying to get "being human" right. And when we leave here, we will be pure Spirit again.

As my life review continued, I got married and had my own children and saw that I was on the edge of repeating the cycle that I had experienced as a child. I was on prescription drugs. I was in the hospital. I was becoming like my mother. And at the same time, this Loving Energy we call God was holding me and let me into Its experience of all this. I felt God's memories of these scenes through God's eyes, just as I had through my grandmother's eyes.

As my life unfolded, I witnessed how severely I had treated myself because that was the behavior shown and taught to me as a child. I realized that the only big mistake I had made in my life was that I had never learned to love myself.

And then I was back here, in this reality.

Following My Heart

I came home after a month. I weighed eighty-three pounds and the body cast weighed thirty pounds. I insisted on seeing a psychiatrist, hoping he would understand what I had experienced. The doctor I saw didn't understand. No one understood NDEs back then, so I realized that I couldn't talk about it. I spent six months in the body cast, thinking about my NDE but not talking about it. Once I was out of the cast and went through some physical therapy to regain my strength, I decided to put the NDE away and follow my heart.

First, I volunteered to work in the emergency room of the hospital where I had been a patient. I was excited that first morning. I put on my volunteer uniform, wishing my pounding headache would subside. My first few hours standing in the corridor of the emergency room, doing what little I was asked to do, was agonizing because of this headache. Then an old woman was brought in on a gurney from an ambulance. She was shivering. I knew she was dying but I didn't know how I knew. A nurse asked me to go over to the warmer and get a few blankets for her. She pointed to what looked like a refrigerator and turned out to be a warmer filled with blankets. I took two over to the shivering woman and spread them over her, one at a time, using my hands to smooth them. Then, to my surprise, something strange started to happen. I felt my headache moving down through my shoulders, draining into my hands and out of my palms, only the sensation wasn't one of pain anymore. It was more like a tingling. I looked at the old woman and she was smiling right into my eyes. She said, "Oh, my dear, I feel a little better." I took her hand in mine and sat down next to her, just content to hold her hand. A few minutes later, she said, "The pain medication is working. I'm out of pain and not so afraid anymore." (My headache was gone too). I sat there for the longest time. Occasionally a nurse or the emergency room doctor walked by and they smiled but they didn't ask me to do any more until much later when the woman was taken to a room.

After that first experience at that hospital, I had many opportunities to be with and touch dying people. Either I searched them out, or the staff asked me to. During my breaks I would go to the rooms of dying people I had met in the emergency room. I felt real when I worked there. And everyone else was real, too. In settings where life and death are on the edge every moment, only the truth is spoken.

My personal life, however, was at the opposite end of the spectrum. My husband, my friends and most family members were caught up in their own games. No one seemed to be communicating honestly. It seemed that what was shown to me in my life review now made me recognize how manipulative our relationships were. We never were able to honestly talk about what we wanted or needed from one another. The most painful part for me was watching the disrespect of each others feelings. I cannot deny that I, too, had once been a part of it, part of the denial and numbness. We used materialism as a way to substitute for authentic living. But now I was different. It wasn't their fault I had changed. The only place I felt real besides the hospital was on a college campus. I realized that I needed to go back to school in order to qualify for some type of health care career.

I graduated a few years later as a respiratory therapist. I loved working in the emergency room and the ICU, where, once again, my patients were telling me about their experiences as they were dying. And those who returned to their bodies told me about their NDEs. I started to write about what I was hearing, calling my topic "the emotional needs of critical-care patients." Surprisingly, I was invited to speak at professional conferences and was published in respiratory therapy journals. The emotional needs of critical care patients was a hot new topic in healthcare during the late 1970s and early 1980s.

Finally, I became a researcher and could start looking for the answers that I so longed to find. Because I was undertaking my research at a university medical school, all kinds of new knowledge became available to me. Now at last I could frame and reframe not only the hundreds of experiences I was studying, but also my own.

Starting to Wake Up

I learned in my life review that the only thing that is real is love, and the only way to share love is by being real. Being real happens when we acknowledge our feelings, the feelings of others and continually share our truth. When we *feel* our feelings and are real, we share our truth out of love. Then our relationship with God and our self is healthy. This relationship is always here and can continue to grow in our lives if we allow it to. This sacred relationship continues to interpret for us what we are doing here, what life may be all about.

When we die, if we re-experience our lives from everyone else's perspective as well as our own, there are only feelings, perceptions and knowledge. We really cannot judge or blame others, because we suddenly understand where we and everyone else is coming from. We only judge here in this earthly reality. When I was with God, I was just learning. The knowledge of what had happened was pouring into me, and I was repeatedly saying my "no wonders!" I came to believe that God doesn't judge but wants us to learn so we won't make the same mistakes again. My experiences showed me that God wants us to stop being fearful and instead, to extend love. Suddenly, I was catapulted out of time and embraced by this whole different way of thinking and being. Just as rapidly, I was back here, wanting to break new ground. I had had a great opportunity, and now I wanted to share it.

Many times over the years since then I have shared this different way of thinking and being with my transitioning clients, friends and relatives that want to experience it, too. I have assisted many in creating their own life reviews while they are still here, using a tape recorder or camcorder.

In fact, what I learned and experienced for myself during my own life review — that a Divine Energy connects all of us — has since orchestrated all of my relationships. Moreover, not only have I witnessed this Spiritual energy on each occasion that I have attended someone during the dying process, but almost every hospice worker I've met during the many talks I have given has also confirmed God's loving energy being present during their own clients' deaths. I've even heard similar remarks from medical staff and relatives regarding births.

To this day, I still feel connected to this Energy through my heart. Within my heart, there is a constant prayer. This prayer forms the background music of every experience I have. When we are connected to God's loving energy, It is the single most powerful force in the universe.

The Power of Humility

When Charles and I started working with Jyoti and Russ, the four of us kept asking, "What moves us up?" or "What throws the switch?" Finally, Charles, with his knowledge of the 12 Steps, suggested, "It's the power of humility." He defined humility as "the openness and willingness to learn more about self, others and if we choose, the God of our understanding." And, of course, as a therapist/healer/Near-Death Experiencer I knew that without that openness and willingness to learn we can't heal and transcend to a life filled with the Energy of our Sacred Person, a life lived from our *natural Soul*. My first "Aha experience" (or sudden insight) in the writing of the humility book ran through me.

In this book I describe what I have learned from my ordinary and Spiritual experiences, especially my life review about living as God planned. You may have experienced some of this too. This is our natural birthright to live as our Natural Soul.

$$\text{X} \quad \text{X} \quad \text{X}$$

We don't have to die or almost die to wake up again to our Soul and to feel the Energy I am referring to above. Experiencing my grandmother holding me in the tunnel created a flood of memories of her love. Each time I thought about her afterwards, each time I tell my story now, I sense that wonderful feeling again of my grandmother's love. Her love moved into me and I felt my Soul. Love does that.

In the next chapter we will talk more about memories and touching Souls with our love.

photo by C.L. Whitfield

Dec. 28, 1998, I am reading to Nicholas 6 hours after he was born. His eyes are wide open staring at this book about trains. Nick is now 10 and still loves trains. His email address is "Nicktheconductor."

Chapter 2

Soul Parenting Remembered

Here's a letter I wrote to Nicholas about 6 weeks before he was born:

November 9, 1998

My Dear Grandson Nicholas,

"I've been thinking about writing you this letter for a long time, at least several weeks. I want to tell you a story of your Mom, Grandpa Charlie and me. The new story we are now sharing is because of you. You've not been born yet but your presence surrounds us. This is your story too. You may not be here yet in our arms, but you are here in your mom's tummy and for sure you have crawled into our hearts.

"You came to me in a special way, one that I didn't expect, about a month before we knew Kate, your mom, was pregnant. I was out shopping with a friend and suddenly I had a "visual flash." I suddenly said, "There's a baby coming. I just met its Soul." I knew you were coming and I also remembered that this was the second time in a few weeks that I felt this special presence of a baby's Soul coming to make me aware of it. I asked your Aunt Beth

and she said, "No." And then I asked my young friend, Carole and she said, "Not yet." I told your Grandpa Charlie, and a few weeks later he talked to your mom over the phone long distance and he then confirmed to me that you were coming, that your mom was having a baby. So, Sweetheart, I feel like I know you already. I'm looking forward to your coming and I am smiling as I think about getting to know Nicholas Christopher Whitfield."

The letter went on for several pages, and I signed it Grandma Barbara. What I didn't know at the time was that Nicholas was going to bring out a part of me I can only call a "Soul Parent." In his presence I could feel my Soul expanding into the privilege and opportunity of becoming a "Spiritual Soul Mother". And I also, in true joy, witnessed Charlie expand into a Spiritual Soul Father. Perhaps this is why we used to call Nicholas "our little guru!"

What does this mean? It's a new concept for someone like me who was taught to believe that our being begins at birth and ends at death. That idea completely changed for me after my encounters with death. It seems almost silly now to believe that a baby's Soul and its conscious awareness begins at birth — and that it doesn't completely develop until months or years after it is born.

Soul Awareness

We are observing that more and more babies today are being born wide awake with full contact to our God source and contact with us, if we are open to it. After two or three years though, they may lose that sensitivity or ability to remember who they are: Souls that have come into physical bodies.

These babies, and all of us, can remember that we are Souls, first and foremost, and will continue to remain so after we "die." We are eternal Souls occupying a finite body. Our body is born and dies. However, our

Soul — that organized conscious energy that sometimes appears as light and other times as an electrical impulse — is eternal. Anyone who has had a Near-Death Experience or other kind of Spiritual experience can tell you that. Everyone who has had a meaningful out-of-body experience says the same thing: *We existed consciously outside our physical body.* This is a kind of experiential proof that we exist *before* and *beyond* our physical self.

The problem is that by the time we turned three, most of us have lost that experiential knowledge, or Soul memory. It could have been different, though. Just imagine how it might have been if a beloved aunt, uncle, or grandparent, or even one or both of our parents, had remained cognizant of the true nature and needs of our Spiritual self. What if we had grown up in the presence of someone who could have looked us in the eye and reminded us of our Soul with a hug, or a song or something that would have perked up our memories as an infant and toddler? If they had rocked us while singing a special song as they cuddled us, or told us we were safe and loved, these people could have been our Soul Parents. They could have kept those Soul memories alive. That was our loss and theirs. Now that we are aware of this, however, we have the opportunity to do it for the little Souls that are entering this dimension now. We can help these beautiful children retain full knowledge of who they are and where they come from, and in so doing we can prevent *Soul amnesia* from setting in.

Soul Amnesia

Most of us forget who we really are because our parents were taught to believe that babies are devoid of the ability to think or be conscious. The belief was that infants cannot even see (except for shadows) when they are born. If *you* were treated as though that were the case, you would not have received any encouragement or stimulation to keep your Soul memories alive. Like the vast majority of us, you would have been brought up to believe this party line, as well as many other untruths, because no one gave us any other choice or assistance to help us remember who we are.

Could it be that all babies — all infants throughout time — have been sensitive and gifted, and we are only now beginning to realize this fact?

Staying connected to who we really are fades into the recesses of our mind, as though it's been tucked behind a stairway in a dimly lit cellar, until later on in life when *something* — a Near-Death Experience perhaps, or meditation, prayer, or other altered states of consciousness or triggers — turns the light on in that recess and we remember. But we don't have to let our children's memories of Unity and our God source fade. We can help them "rehearse" our memory of Home.

The term "rehearsal" refers to a way psychologists explain taking material from short term memory (which lasts seconds to minutes) and placing it into long term memory, where it will last years or longer. Rehearsal is the deliberate act of repeating the material in various ways, from speaking to writing. For preverbal children (infants and toddlers) this doesn't work well. What works best for them is cuddling (not tickling),[3] singing and an attitude of Unconditional Love that is continuously reflected in the way we look at a child and treat them.

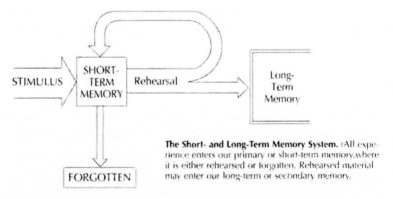

The Short- and Long-Term Memory System. (All experience enters our primary or short-term memory, where it is either rehearsed or forgotten. Rehearsed material may enter our long-term or secondary memory.

(Whitfield, C.L. *Memory and Abuse* 1995 page 16)

---

[3] Tickling invades a person's personal physical boundaries and may be abusive to some children.

Charlie and I have a blended family. Charlie's biological daughter is Kate. My biological daughter is Beth and I have two sons, Steven and Gary. Together we now have nine grandchildren. They have each taught Charlie and me about being open to possibilities. When our children were pregnant with our grandchildren, they invited us to place our hands upon their swelling bellies and patiently waiting for delightful kicks, followed in late pregnancy by the amazing feelings of slow restricted stretches. They also invited us to talk to the babies in utero. These young, soon-to-be mothers also held stereo headsets and pillow speakers in place over their bellies to sooth their unborn babies with classical and meditative music. (They never played loud or harsh music and they didn't use alcohol or other drugs, including nicotine, which are toxic to the fetus).

Nicholas' Birth

Kate did extensive research on ways of birthing. She told us she wanted to birth her baby naturally with the Bradley Method.[4] She explained to us that the kind of pregnancy, labor, and birth our children experience has a profound and lifelong effect on their health, including their mental, emotional, and physical health. The Bradley Method attempts to give babies the best possible start in life by teaching how to have a *natural pregnancy* and a natural childbirth. Usually the father is the "coach."

Kate asked us to become her coaches because Nicholas's father was now out of the picture. We attended two-hour classes once a week in

---

[4] The Bradley Method® teaches natural childbirth and views birth as a natural process. The method holds that most women with proper education, preparation, and the help of a loving and supportive coach can be taught to give birth naturally. The Bradley Method is a system of natural labor techniques in which a woman and her coach play an active part. It is a simple method of increasing self-awareness, teaching a woman how to deal with the stress of labor by tuning in to her own body. The Bradley Method encourages mothers to trust their bodies using natural breathing, relaxation, nutrition, exercise, and education.

Relaxation is the key during labor. It is the safest and most effective way to reduce unnecessary pain and to handle any pain that you do experience. The Bradley Method encourages mothers to trust their bodies (and emphasizes relaxed abdominal breathing and relaxation throughout labor). For more information on Bradley® classes see www.bradleybirth.com.

the evenings. Charlie's training as a physician and mine as a respiratory therapist didn't teach us what we learned in these weekly sessions.

We learned to help Kate find comfort in a variety of ways from three or four pillows placed strategically while she practiced relaxing into the pain — and I mean *relaxing* — not leaving her body, not dissociating — but using the pain to take her deeper into a relaxed state where her muscles would let go instead of freeze up against pain. We experimented with heat packs that were warmed in microwave ovens. We even did role-playing to teach us how to stand firm and say, "No" if the staff would try to convince us to allow them to give her pain medication. Writing her own birth plan, which was read and followed by the hospital staff, was really empowering for Kate. She and we went into this birth educated and prepared. The Bradley Method (and other drug-free birthing) is an amazing way to deliver a new Soul into this dimension. The proof is in the level of conscious awareness that the mother and the baby have at birth.

Kate is barely five feet tall and normally weighs 100 pounds. Nick came into this world at a little over nine pounds. She was in labor for 33 hours. To quote our midwife, Joan, who delivered Nick, "Any other woman would have been begging for a C-section ten hours ago — and we would have given it to her!"

During the 33 hours of labor, there wasn't that euphoric mood that I expected from the videos they had showed us in the classes. This was hard work and took concentration. Sometimes we helped Kate into a warm bathtub where she could moan through a contraction and then sleep in between. I sat on the floor next to the tub and held her hand. All I could do when she slept was study her face and realize how much I loved her. Our midwife came in often to check on her and commented on the love she could feel between us.

When Kate was nine centimeters dilated, her cervix still had a small lip. Joan helped push the rim aside and soon Kate was fully dilated and ready for the second stage of labor. She pushed for over three hours.

Finally, Nick's head crowned. I was holding one of Kate's legs up and applying pressure back, and a nurse was doing the same to her other leg. Our keeping her legs back helped her push. I could see Nick's head crowning. He had been in the birth canal for so long that his head had become elongated. I remember thinking of Dan Ackroyd and Jane Curtain as the "Coneheads". Was our baby being born deformed? I started cringing inside.

Then I fainted!

I'm not proud of fainting, but what happened next was incredible. After I fainted, Kate's contractions stopped. Everyone in the room realized that as long as I was out of commission, her body seemed to stop the delivery. The nurse watching the monitor said to Kate, "Your contractions are taking a little break." Kate and everyone attending her were stunned. What an amazing example of how we humans/Souls are connected, all the time.

I heard a voice whisper in my ear as I lay on the cold floor, "If you ever tell anyone about this, I will report you to the floor police!" And then someone was waving something awful smelling under my nose. Someone helped me up and into a rocking chair. I recognized him as one of the physicians from the OB practice. "How did you get here so fast?" I asked. "Timing is everything!" he answered. "I was just walking by and peeked in to check on how you were all doing. I watched you go down."

From the edge of the rocking chair I leaned closer to get a better view. With the doctor kneeling beside me, together we watched Nicholas' head emerge during the final push. The doctor smiled and remarked that he'd never seen a baby being born from this point of view, in other words, this time he was an observer.

Nicholas was suddenly out. The staff immediately placed him on Kate's chest and then placed a stocking cap on his head and covered him with a warm blanket. After the cord stopped pulsing and the baby transitioned into breathing, Charlie cut the cord. Kate and Nick's faces were no more than five or six inches apart and they were staring into each other's eyes. The gaze was beautiful. No one said a word. This was incredibly powerful. We all stared at them. He was wide-eyed, peaceful, and totally awake. There was no crying from him. He looked like he was in awe. We could almost hear him thinking, *Oh! Hi! So this is what you look like, Mom!*

A nurse came in to bathe Nick. Kate had signed papers earlier disallowing them from putting antibiotic drops in his eyes. Those drops are too toxic and they sting. They were originally created to prevent infections. This happens only in vaginal births when the mother *has* an infection. Physicians know that. It is otherwise useless, including in C-sections since the baby does not even go through the birth canal. But they keep doing it, because the legal system makes them.

I stood guard during Nick's bathing to make sure no one slipped the drops in. I also had our camcorder going the whole time. Charlie used his hands as a shield to protect Nicholas' eyes from the light of the baby warmer during his sponge bath. I continued filming Nick afterwards. He raised his wrinkled newborn hands, and I said "Oh, Nicholas, your hands look like raisins!"

Then Charlie jokingly said, "He's already being emotionally abused." At this point, to my amazement, Nick lifted his hand to the camera with his middle finger extended!

Signing

Over the next several months, Nick taught us that babies can communicate through sign language, even though the communication centers in their brains may not be ready to use speech. That first "finger" Nick gave me might have been a mere coincidence, but the others that followed — asking for more food, telling us he was finished, wanting to be held, wanting to get out of his high chair, telling us he was over-stimulated and needed some peace (by turning away and refusing to have eye contact with us) — were all signs that he either showed to us or we taught to him after we had read books on signing.[5]

The next two years were filled with days with Nick while Kate worked. This was a special time for Charlie and me. In our 50s, we were given the opportunity to be very close with our "little guru," as we called him. He taught us much and we attended him with love. Then, when Nick was a little over two, he and Kate moved back to Colorado.

Memory

When Nick was six years old, he told Kate that he had a visual memory of sitting on "Grandma Barbara's lap" and playing with my keys. He described the curly red plastic attachment I use to keep my keys around my wrist. Kate and Nick moved back to Colorado four years before that. He never sees my keys. This is a memory from infancy that demonstrates "rehearsal." We could speculate, that as a preverbal infant and toddler, he was rehearsing kinesthetically and visually. Baby Nicholas played with my keys and the red "bracelet" attached for more times then I can count. They seemed to sooth him when he was teething. He was on my lap leaning into me and chewing on the red curly plastic, as I gently rubbed his back. We repeated this act over and over again, and it went into his long-term memory. Later telling Kate about the event helped him to rehearse it. When I asked him about it months later, he explained the memory to me. Our eyes met and we could easily imagine that peaceful mood again. We shared a memory of tenderness and compassion for what had been a teething baby. This moment we shared is some of what I am trying to explain when I refer to keeping babies' Soul memories alive.

---

[5] Baby Signs by Linda Acredolo PhD and Susan Goodwyn PhD These books are excellent because they are written for the babies. On each page is a picture of a baby's face and a simple gesture, based on American Sign Language (ASL), that resembles objects, activities or emotions. Also included is a poster to place on the refrigerator or somewhere where the whole family can see it. "http://www.babysigns.com" www.babysigns.com

Seven years ago when Kate returned to Colorado, she met Andrew. They fell in love and married. Kate and Nick are now living in the Rocky Mountains with Andrew, his son Thomas who is a year and a half older then Nick and lives with them part time, Anna, who is four years old, and Jonathan, who is three. Anna and Jonathan are also Bradley babies.

Recently, we received an email from Kate that ended with this paragraph:

"Last night I showed Andrew the slide show I made when I left Atlanta. He loved it. Lots of memories (or "re-memberies" as Nick used to call them) came back. I'm so happy we all got to share in Nick's birth. How did you know to invite me? My life will always be special because of it."

Having Kate and Nick with us gave us the opportunity to live almost constantly with a higher perception of life and a more Soulful relationship with ourselves. We found a closer relationship with each other and God, in addition to a closer relationship with Kate and Nick. A little over two years later, when Kate courageously moved back to Colorado, we used prayer to help us let go, and we stayed aware during our grieving. This moved us into a new way of being that we couldn't have predicted. Perhaps as parents we were too busy to have the kind of experiences we now continue to have with Nick and all our grandchildren. I know that when Nicholas and I gaze into each other's eyes now, and perhaps eternally, that gaze will remind us both of our Soul nature.

photo by C.L. Whitfield

Kate and Nick gazing at about an hour after his birth

The phenomenon of Gazing

My daughter, Beth, delivered Ethan Dennis Graves by C-section. We weren't allowed to be present in the delivery room, but within a few minutes of his delivery he was wheeled out with Eddie, Ethan's new dad, walking next to the crib and holding his little hand. Within moments they settled into a new baby nursery where we and Eddie's parents could watch through a window. Eddie, seated on a stool, stared into Ethan's face continuously while stroking his arm and face. The only thing that could stop him was the nurse's invitation to ask each one of us to come in, one at a time, to look at Ethan. And what did each one of us do? We gazed into his face and stroked his skin. The most remarkable thing happened. He gazed back into our faces. We were transfixed by his gaze.

When Beth came back into her room, we all moved in with her and took turns gazing into Ethan's face. This just happened naturally. Sometimes he slept and sometimes he stared back. When Ethan was in bed with Beth, if she wasn't holding him, they were both on their sides, facing each other, with their faces about six inches apart. Their gaze was obvious and profound. Beth then naturally stroked his skin.

25

Here's what science has now learned about newborn babies and gazing: From birth, human infants prefer to look at faces that engage them in mutual gaze, and from an early age, healthy babies show enhanced neural processing of direct gaze. The exceptionally early sensitivity to mutual gaze demonstrated in these studies is a major foundation for the later development of social skills.[6]

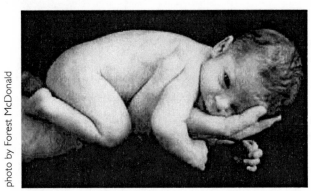

photo by Forest McDonald

New born baby Ethan resting in the hand of his father, Ed.

Soul Bonding with our Babies

When I looked into Ethan's face and cuddled him in my arms, even when he was just hours old, I would repeat to him over and over, "Welcome to Earth! You are safe. You have wonderful parents! We're so happy you are here!"

Every night, before bed, Beth sang to him:
    "I see the moon, and the moon sees me.
    The moon sees somebody I'd like to see.
    God Bless the moon and God bless me
    and God bless the somebody I'd like to see.
    It seems to me that God above

---

[6] Farroni T, Csibra G, Simion F, Johnson MH 2002 Eye contact detection in humans from birth. Centre for Brain and Cognitive Development, School of Psychology, University of London, Malet Street, London WC1E 7HX, United Kingdom

created Ethan for me to love.
He picked you out from all the rest
because he knew I'd love Ethan best."

And I sing that to Ethan, too, as it is the same song I sang to my three children, to Nicholas, and to all my other grandchildren now. The first time Kate heard me sing it to Nick she got very excited because her mom used to read her a similar poem. There is something very bonding about singing; it helps to keep our Soul memories intact.

Besides song, getting down on the floor to "just be" with a baby or a child at any age creates a bond that lasts a lifetime. Eye contact is important, even if we are already playing with them. We build a tower with blocks and look into their little faces. Twenty minutes of eye contact while playing is comparable to hours of play without eye contact. Once the children are mobile, whatever they want to do we can do with them. It's their preference. Bonding doesn't happen if they have to follow what we want. Bonding happens when we "play" according to their preferences.

The bonus for us is that through their eyes we get to see the world afresh and we can remember our childlike self. Children can teach us more about this kind of awe if we are open to learning it.

My son Gary was maybe three of four when he dragged me down to the creek to see "Fishies Mommy." Armed with a bucket and strainer, we walked two houses away from ours and were leaning over into the creek looking at tadpoles, thousands of them. Walking back hand in hand, he chattered excitedly about his fishies. This was the first spring he was old enough to appreciate all this. Or was it? Could it have been the first spring I was "young" enough to get down to his level?

Gary stood looking in the bucket while I crouched on my knees on the front porch. The tadpoles were truly amazing to stare at. The next thing I knew, his father was pulling up the drive. I hadn't even started dinner. I was totally transfixed for how long I do not know. And time really didn't matter. Gary showed me awe. For the first time since my Near-Death Experience, I realized that the "bubbles" I had seen during my life review (see page 7) were available here in this dimension, too.

Frankie and Mike

Frankie and Michael are twins who recently graduated from high school at the top of their class. When they were about two and a half years old, their mom and I took them to the beach. I was quietly sitting in the water about six inches deep. Frankie spontaneously sat down in my lap and rested her ear on my chest, right over my heart. She sat still and relaxed for a long time, much longer than I would expect a toddler to sit. It was a special moment outside of time that I will never forget.

Frankie and Mike's mom, Robynne, told me this story, "when the twins were about three and a half, the day was cold and rainy and the twins were stuck inside and bored. To reduce the frustration caused by their pent-up energy, I created a 'high tea.' I set the coffee table with a linen tablecloth and napkins. For the first time in their lives, they drank from fine china cups, with saucers, using silver spoons. Their cups were half full of hot black tea, with cream and sugar. The formality of the occasion captivated them. As always, Francesca embraced the opportunity, and provided an appropriately serious conversation starter. Sitting in her tiny wooden rocking chair, she leaned back and took a breath. 'If we lose our eyes, we cannot see.' That is when Michael answered, 'If we lose our eyes, we see with our hearts. That's what God says.' All three of us sat in silence and absorbed this."

That was about fifteen years ago, and having known the twins personally for that long, I can testify that they were exceptional children then and are exceptional teenagers now.

Robynne told me recently, "Every step of the way I have reminded Mike and Frankie that they are eternal and that time is an illusion." And then she added, "If moms and dads choose to prioritize Spirituality, they can fulfill the role of Soul parents, too.

This mom is referring to relating Soulfully to her children. The table below illustrates the difference between relating to someone from our ego versus relating through our Soul.

Voice of the Ego or Voice of the Soul

Ego Traits	Soul Traits
Flatters	Informs
Commands	Suggests
Demands	Guides
Tests	Nudges
Chooses for you	Leaves choice to you
Imprisons	Empowers
Promotes dependence	Promotes independence
Intrudes	Respects
Pushes	Supports
Excludes	Includes
Instills fear	Promotes well-being
Becomes bored easily	Realizes peace when doing nothing
Is status oriented	Is free and open
Judges	Accepts Individuality
Demands obedience	Encourages growth and development
Implies having ultimate authority	Recognizes a Higher Power
Offers shortcuts	Offers integration
Seeks personal gratification	Extends Unconditional Love
Self-righteous	Humility

© B Whitfield 2008

photo by Andrew Hart

Here we are at Kate and Andrew's in the Rocky Mountains. Kate is holding Jonathan, Me and Nick, and Charlie holding Anna.

Unconditional Love

In my Near-Death Experience, my grandmother held me in the tunnel. That holding brought back all the memories of how much we loved each other. All my memories of her, all the memories of wonderful loving times we spent together, came flooding back. All the toxic pain (also called negative ego or false self, which will be explained further in the next chapter) of this lifetime fell away. I felt whole again and I remembered my Soul, and now I can draw on that memory whenever I want or need to. I remember my grandmother, and I feel her love igniting my Soul. This was a type of experiential *rehearsal*. She gave me that gift.

In my childhood, my parents couldn't give me what I needed. Besides my grandmother, I also had an aunt and uncle that were my Soul advocates. I went over to their house every weekend to escape and have fun. My aunt and uncle were not only attentive to me, their very look felt warm and welcoming. These three people — my grandmother, my aunt and my uncle — were my Soul parents. I could do no wrong in their eyes. They loved me unconditionally. They saved my Soul.

My aunt and my grandmother have made their transition to the other side. But I find this same relationship in the here and now with my grandchildren and with other children that come my way, even the ones I don't know and may not formally meet. A child being carried past me or wheeled by in a stroller looks into my face and I purposely have total eye contact with them. If there is a pause, I smile a wide smile, and I think "Welcome to Planet Earth!" If there is an opportunity, I start a conversation with them and they respond.

Our community pool is a wonderful place to have contact with little kids. Their mothers often say that the children's grandparents live in other cities so they welcome the attention of others for their children.

It's so easy to give children unconditional love and it makes a huge difference to them even decades from now. The little ones coming into

31

this dimension now are open and sensitive. Tokens of our love, from the slightest glance, to the biggest hug, are their birthright and our privilege to deliver.

Chapter 3

The Adventure of Our Soul

God has a dream
And the dream comes true —
Each time one of us
Awakens.
     BHW

In his foreword to my second book, Spiritual Awakenings, Charles Whitfield asks several important questions, including: "Who am I?" "What am I doing here?" "Where am I going?" And "How can I get any peace?"

While the definitive answers to these questions will remain a Divine Mystery, Charlie has attempted to begin creating some understanding by constructing a map of the Self.

Map of the Self (adapted from C. Whitfield)

Higher Power (God, Goddess, All-That-Is)

↕

"Sacred Person"   **Higher Self (Guardian Angel, Spirit)**

↕

Soul (True Self, Child Within)

false self

positive ego   **negative ego**

Other names for the True Self — who we really are — include the Real or Existential Self, the Human Heart, the Soul and the Child Within. They are all the same because they are our *true identity*. Just as an acorn contains the potential for its identity, a giant oak tree, we, too, contain the potential at birth for our Soul to develop to its fullest in this lifetime. If a newborn baby is given everything it needs as it grows and develops — a loving bond with caregivers, mirroring of feelings, stimulation to learn, praise, healthy role models, etc. — then this baby will likely grow up to fulfill all of its potential, realizing and experiencing its natural connection to its Divine Nature.

This Divine Nature that we call Higher Self can also be called Guardian Angel, Atman, Buddha Nature, Christ Consciousness or simply Self. Both of these, our Soul/True Self and our Higher Self, are intimately connected to our Higher Power, which we may call God/Goddess/All-That-Is. And, this God of the entire Universe is not only with us, it is also within us.

Sacred Person

This relationship — True Self, Higher Self and God — is such an important relationship that we can view it as being one person, which we can call the *Sacred Person*. When we are in alignment, when we are our authentic True Self connected to our Higher Self and God, we are no longer a human being hoping for a Spiritual experience. *We are a Spiritual Being — a Soul* living through a human body. We may even experience the presence of God's Divine Energy, which some call Holy Spirit, Chi, Ki, or Ruach Ha Kadosh. Each religion has a name for this Divine Energy. Regardless of whether we are or are not religious, this Divine Energy is always with us, patiently waiting for us to realize Its presence. During births and during deaths, Its presence is easier to recognize if we are *being* our Sacred Person: our Soul connected to our Higher Self, which is then connected to God. And, every time we need Divine Energy's assistance, all we need do is ask. My experiences have shown me time and again, this Divine Energy is always with us. All we have to do is ask for help and get our ego out of the way so the Energy can come through and work through us. Many others have told me that, even though they didn't believe any of this, they had the intention to help someone else and were then surprised to realize "something" was working through them.

Ego

As part of the Divine Mystery, my Soul makes or constructs an assistant to help me as I live out this human experience. We can call this sidekick the ego. Ego can be positive or negative. When the ego is helpful to us, such as in screening, sorting and handling many aspects of our internal and external reality, we can call it positive ego. My positive ego is writing this. Your positive ego is reading it. Positive ego balances our checkbook, keeps us on time for appointments, etc. When it tries to take over and control our life, however, it becomes negative ego, also known as false self or co-dependent self. This part of us believes we are annihilated when we die. It may believe in the Universe as an intellectual head trip. And it often believes it is a victim. (See Voice of the Ego or Voice of the Soul on page 29).

An easy way to tell if you are in your ego or being your True Self is to wait until you are doing nothing. As you relax into "doing nothing," are you feeling bored? Or is there a quiet feeling of peaceful being deep within you? If you are bored, it's likely your ego complaining. If you are peaceful, this is your True Self just "being." When I realize I feel bored, I try saying a spontaneous prayer of gratitude. My heart/Soul may scan all I am grateful for and this may bring me back to a state of peaceful being.

Peaceful being is the state the mystics have searched for and written about for millennia. Enjoy being in this peace. Choosing peace over the ego is a goal of meditation. Calling on it during our busy lives is a sacred privilege we are all entitled to have. Meditation helps with this whole process, especially letting go of ego.

What is Real?

As I relate the stories in my book *Final Passage: Sharing the Journey as this Life Ends*, I occasionally pause and explain this difference that happens as someone is preparing to make their transition. Their ego is becoming weaker and their Soul stronger. Observing this helps the reader to recognize the switching back and forth between their Soul or Real Self and their ego or false self. The longer I have worked with transitioning people the more aware I have become of an almost "flipping" mechanism that happens. When unsafe people are around, my patients stay in their ego. Bring in someone they deeply love and feel safe with and they move over and settle into their Soul. As a caregiver I can usually help them to remain in their Soul when we are alone or with safe others.

Being with someone who is dying provides an opportunity like no other to help us learn how to practice being real and feeling connected. Whether we are the person dying or the person assisting in the transition, this process is a chance to step out of our egos and practice being our Soul.

A *Course in Miracles* says in its introduction:
> *What is real cannot be threatened*
> *What is unreal does not exist.*
> *Herein lies the peace of God.*

What is real is God and God's world — the world of the Soul and Sacred Person. The ego and its world is not real, and therefore, in the grand scheme of the Mystery, does not exist. Herein, when we make this differentiation, lies our peace and serenity. By learning to differentiate between identifying with our True Self and our false self, we learn the way to peace and serenity. We might even say we are learning to "stand in the Light of our Soul."

Some of these ideas may be hard to grasp. Identifying with our Soul, our Real Self — and not our body — is a strange concept in a world in which we are being bombarded with messages about the way we look. Magazines, television, and movies tell us that we're not young enough, thin enough or firm enough. Our society bombards us with materialistic messages that keep us locked in our body and our possessions as our only identity. In our world today, there are many people who don't know about their Souls. They have become distracted by materialism and the media which defines for them what reality is. They have fallen asleep to the Real World.

Much of the time people who are "asleep" find that, when they are preparing for their transition, they wake up to their true identity and realize that they are not just their body before they die. They let go of the image of themselves as just their body and at the same time realize they are not their ego. They wake up to their Spiritual nature, which is their Soul. Sometimes, as I meet a patient for the first time, they will tell me that. There is a sense of joy at the knowledge that this worn-out or diseased body is going to drop away and release them back into wholeness.

Leaving our bodies

My colleagues and I have interviewed hundreds of Near-Death Experiencers and we all say the same thing. We were not upset to lose our body and this incarnation once we realized that we were still who we are and that the "thing" we were leaving behind was painful, cumbersome and inhibiting. There was often a sense of, "Oh! So that one's over! Now I can get some rest while I heal and start again anew."

If our death was not sudden, if there was sufficient time to realize that we were dying, then, yes, it often was painful detaching from the people we love. But once we had left our bodies, we were not so upset about leaving. Many of us reported being joyful. We felt peace. Many of us became ecstatic as we moved toward the Light.

Our problems began when we had to return to the physical plane. We liked leaving our toxic pain or egos behind and coming home to our Self; we felt real again and we felt the connection to our Higher Self and God. We liked more fully experiencing who we really are — our Sacred Person. Once we were back here on Earth in our body, however, we had to struggle because our loved ones and our society wanted us to resume our old roles, which meant putting our egos back on or being our false self.

Sometimes, when people are dying, this mechanism of dropping the ego and being real begins long before the dying process is complete. Those of us assisting them have an easy time because all we need to do is be *real*. Being real invites our attention to focus on the Divine Energy that is really orchestrating everything, and we can release into the dance of life and death. We become aware of the cycle that the Eastern religions have always referred to: birth-life-death — learning, resting, healing — birth-life-death. Souls come in and Souls go out. The ego and the body die, but we — our Essence that we here term our Soul or True Self — continues our journey of growth and transformation. Physics confirms this in the first law of thermodynamics, which in part says that energy can be converted from one form to another, but it cannot be created or destroyed.

Final Passage

Birth is an experience of celebration. Death can be, too. I am not trying to get your hopes up about what it is like to die. My book, *Final Passage*, is realistically written, containing some stories about people who never transformed to anything higher. At the same time, however, it also contains stories of what is possible when Spirit transforms suffering. When we are being real we share our Truth. Being real and sharing our Truth "flips" our consciousness into a deeper dimension that is Spiritual, where suffering is only what is happening to the body, not to us. Suffering is about fearing our pain. When we make room for Spirit, we stop fearing and the suffering dissolves.

The stages of birth-life-death cycle are beautifully designed to occur at exactly the right time with the assistance of God's Divine Energy. Each one of us creates or designs our timing so that it is not one minute before or one minute after the appropriate moment. Our ego can do none of this. Our Soul/True Self, in concert with our Higher Self and with God, is creating our timetable. Our ego is the victim of our dying. Ego is the pain of trying to hold on. Our Soul can orchestrate our death with grace.

Our Soul's nature is to create. There is a formless part of ourselves, like the part of the acorn that holds the oak tree that creates our personality, ego and image. Its nature is to create. If we identify with the **creation** — our bodies, ego, image — we will suffer in life and in death. If we identify with the **creator** — our Soul, our Higher Self and God — we will end our suffering. At this level, we go behind the ego chatter and we are free.

No matter how Spiritual or free we become, as we move toward death there may still be some moments or elements of physical pain if we decide not to take any medication. We may experience the pain, but not the suffering that we created by **resisting the pain**. If we examine our pain closely, what emerges is the knowledge that, in part, pain sculpts who we are becoming. We are "becoming" throughout our entire life, and this includes every moment of the dying process.[7]

Examining Pain

Looking back on our lives, would we give up our pain? I wouldn't. I spent seven months in a full body cast. I wore one cast for a month before

---

[7] See Whitfield C, A Gift To Myself . Read the section on Stage Two "Learning to tolerate emotional pain"

surgery, and then I wore an identical one for six months after surgery. The cast began at my armpits and ended at my knees. At 30 pounds, it weighed over a third of my body weight. The cast I wore before surgery taught me how to tolerate the post-surgery cast while I was still strong enough to learn the tricks of survival. The worst part of the one-month pre-surgery cast was that it showed me what was to come, and I felt full of dread while suspended in the Stryker frame Circle Bed. I was in that Circle Bed for almost a month, dreading the next cast. Then, for six months I was again encased in plaster that restricted my every move. That period of my life deepened my knowledge of myself a thousand-fold.

Even if I had never had a Near-Death Experience, that body cast would still have changed me profoundly. This rock-like enclosure kept me in the moment, and it kept me real. There was no place to hide. Being real every second of every day brought me closer to God again. I watched all my defenses drop away. Every new pain brought on by the cast brought me closer to realizing my True Self. If we can recognize this, if we can recognize our physical pain as an anchor that keeps us in the moment, we can release our desire to cling to our false self. The moment we look to see where we are clinging, and let go, we are released again to be our True Self. Pain can be the vehicle to cause us to release attachments, defenses and ego.

As we die, there may be denial, pain and fear. How much of this can we transmute by reframing it as suffering, clinging and resisting, and then releasing it? How much can we transform?

Spirit transforms suffering. When we connect with this part of our Soul we are being real. Being real and sharing our Truth moves, transitions, or "flips" our consciousness into a deeper dimension that is Spiritual, where suffering is only what is happening to the body, not to us. This may be hard to understand intellectually but can be intuited by sensing this from our hearts. There is a moment of possibility where consciousness can so jump from suffering to celebration.

Flipping

The ego suffers
By resisting pain.
The Soul learns
By metabolizing it.

The ego believes
It will die.
The Soul knows
It returns to another reality.

The ego ages in linear time.
The Soul becomes radiant
Here, in Eternal time.

The ego is isolated and
Feels alone.
The Soul knows it is part
Of something much Bigger.

The ego lives stressed.
The Soul relaxes into life.

The ego is addicted to drama
To grow more of itself.
The Soul lives with peace of mind.

The ego believes enlightenment
Is not real.
The Soul knows that a new enlightenment
Comes with each resolution
Of each problem that life brings us.

The ego suffers.
The Soul celebrates.

Ego and Soul have one thing in common:
When they are in action
They grow more of themselves.

It's our choice
Every single time.

   BHW

Time

When we are functioning from our Soul we realize that we have gone through a huge time shift or a different perception of time. We realize experientially that linear time is a construct of our intellect and has moved us to living on a horizontal line. With natural Spirituality we are connected in a vertical relationship with Spirit, and we experience time in a vertical fashion, which reveals a sense of the eternal Now. We are like the giant oak tree: roots planted firmly in our physical body and our Soul/Spirit reaching, like huge branches, stretching up to meet the heavens. We still meet our appointments "on time" but our perception of time changes to give us a peaceful experience whereby we can focus on the task at hand and be totally present with it.

We have worked hard to heal our wounds, and in their place comes so much more than we could have ever predicted. At this time in our own evolution, gratitude and humility give us a constant renewal that allows us to feel the overflowing abundance of the Universe. All our striving to become who God meant us to be happens. As our physical being and our Soul become one, our journey and destination become one, demonstrating the truth about duality and polarity. It was all an illusion. We are One, and separation collapses. We re-member who we are and we are home. Even the belief in heaven *after* this lifetime recedes as we experience creating heaven here.

Timeless Zone

I'm walking around in this reality
Somewhat confused!
I have resided in more than one
And physical reality puzzles me more
Than the "altered states" I have played in.

Confusions arise here
As beliefs drop away.
All the dichotomies come crashing down
And opposites dance on the same continuum.

Sometimes, not to be recommended,
While going through pain.
But probably the quickest way to go.

To Exist is not to live
But just "to exist."
To live, really LIVE,
We have to dive in
And swim around in IT!

When the Doors of perception
Finally clear,
The awareness of living in the NOW.
Timeless NOW.

So this is "Cosmic Consciousness."
First it comes in flashes,
Then interludes.
Finally, an understanding of
GRACE.

And what GOD is—
Where I wind up at the end of all my words.

BHW

*If people can look into each other's eyes with love
And truth in their hearts, anything is possible.*

BHW

Chapter 4

The Love of Our Life

I just watched another "chic flick." Hollywood's rendition of romance is fun on a cold January night. We can curl up with a blanket and a bowl of popcorn and laugh and cry with our heroine. Romance on a screen warms our hearts and releases some chemicals through our tears that leave our bodies relaxed and our Souls glowing. Unfortunately, it also sets up us naïve ones for a big thump when we don't find romance like Cameron Diaz or Meg Ryan.

I married too young the first time. Ours was a "high school romance" complete with sock hops and James Dean. We married a year out of high school for me and just as he was graduating from college. I didn't start college until I was 38, when it felt like our three kids were ready for a college student mom. My high school sweetheart and I divorced when we had been married 23 years. We had grown apart. I don't recommend picking a life partner when you are in the 9th grade.

In the middle of our divorce, I moved to Connecticut to assist Bruce Greyson with the research on Near-Death Experiences. I had never lived alone, moving out of my parent's house the day I married. Now at the age of 42 I found myself in an apartment in Hartford, Connecticut. My car was broken into three or four times. The bag ladies on the street in front of our building were a constant reminder of the future I had chosen, one that had no security. Research assistants could be "pink slipped" or let go any time that funding ran out, only to be rehired when new monies were received.

But living in the city alone in an old apartment building seemed so romantic. Didn't Sigourney Weaver do it in *Ghostbusters!* (I had watched that movie countless times during our initial separation. It was held over at the dollar movie theater near our house). *Ghostbusters* kept me laughing during the initial crazy time at the beginning of a gut-wrenching, long-term marriage break up.

Dating was not one of my favorite activities during the next seven years. I had to stop setting myself up for every new date being the possible "love of my life" or "the man of my dreams."

I met Charlie in 1985, the same year I moved to Connecticut. I was at a conference in Washington DC and he was there too. There was a panel discussion at the end of the day with two of my colleagues, Ken Ring and Stan Grof (with whom I had just taken a one-week workshop). My question, which was lengthy and complex, drew parallels between the two men's work. Charlie came up afterwards and introduced himself. About two or three times a year for the next five years, Charlie would call me at the university and ask me research questions. I would give him the best answer I could from our research and then follow up by mailing him copies of research papers that backed up my answers, always with a short handwritten note.

In 1990, to introduce my first book, *Full Circle,* I appeared on Larry King Live one Monday night. Charlie, who had just come home from his office, flipped on the TV and there I was. He told me later that just the week before, he and a single friend of his were sitting out on San Francisco Bay, praying together that each of them would find a long-term healthy relationship.

The Friday before my appearance on The Larry King Show, as I lit my Sabbath candles, I said a prayer along the same lines as Charlie's prayer. I looked through the two dancing flames and realized that I was alone.

(Usually, my two sons who lived with me were there, but not that night). The space between the two flames somehow let me know that this was a direct line to God. I quickly said the rote prayers and then this came out: "Okay, God. I'm ready. (Long pause) Dear God, please send me someone kind. And, someone smart. As smart as me." (I was getting tired of hiding my intelligence on first and second dates. Third dates usually were a disaster because I wasn't hiding anymore!) Then I took a deep breath and I knew this next part took a lot of courage. I asked for someone I "deserve."

Working in a Psych department and spending years working on my own inner healing process made me cringe as I asked for someone I deserved. That meant something romantic, but that also meant someone who would match me in the areas that still needed to be worked on. God knows how much shadow/false self or ego I have left! I don't! But I asked for someone I deserved because: it just popped out.

When Charlie sat down and watched me on Larry King Live, he realized as the show was over that he was coming up to Hartford the next weekend to speak at an ACoA (Adult Children of Alcoholics) Conference. He called me on the Wednesday after Larry King and invited me to dinner after his talk on Friday night. I sat by the phone, stunned. After we hung up I asked, sitting alone in my kitchen, "Does It work this fast?"

I had to tell Charlie I couldn't have dinner with him because I was treating a chemotherapy patient with massage and energy balancing every evening that week. I said I could meet him for lunch the next day. Friday morning, my patient called to say her Friday treatment had just been cancelled. So I came to his talk anyway that evening. The rest is history. We dated back and forth for a year from Connecticut and Baltimore, Maryland and then we moved in together. To test this whole scary thing called "commitment," we lived together for three years and then we made the big plunge, which as I write, was over 15 years ago. I would like to report that I've been Meg Ryan for the last 18 years and Charlie somewhere between Paul Newman and Jude Law.

Not so!

"Someone I deserved" has filled my life and his with many sentimental moments that we both deserve, but the honest down to earth truth is that we have had no choice but to work really hard to make this "thing" work. "Smitten" and "Romance" are the first 1% of any relationship, and then the real relationship work begins. So where is "the love of my life?" It is Charlie but it is Charlie in relationship to something much bigger than him… or me. Our hard work at making our relationship work, "getting down" and learning the "art" of marriage, has brought us both to an everyday understanding of who the love of our life is.

Let's back up for a few minutes to a dream I had a few weeks after our dinner in Hartford back in 1990.

Our Sacred Person

My dream took me to the first hotel suite where I sat and talked with Charlie. There was a sitting room with two sofas and a round dining table surrounded by four chairs. He and I went into this room to sit and talk, and there at the table was a little man who resembled Desmond Tutu (whom I had heard speak in 1987 and was enchanted with). Because this dream was a "lucid" dream, I felt as though I was awake and had the capacity to think during it. I thought, "This is our combined negative ego/false self or our combined shadow. Charlie and I have a small amount of work to do together because this is a symbolic small man at our table [please God!]. I was grateful this man at "our" table wasn't a Sumo wrestler!

Still in the dream, Charlie took my hand and together we walked out into the hall and searched the corridor for the beginning of a tour. The halls turned into a maze that looked like we were in the clerical/office part of a factory. Finally, we saw a light on in one of the doorways and walked in. A man walked up to us as we stood at the counter and he asked if he could help. "We're here for the tour," we said.

48

He answered, "You're here for the Power Plant Tour."

"Yes. How do we get there?"

"Follow me. I'll show you the way." And he walked around the counter and walked out the door.

Following this man and still holding Charlie's hand, I asked him, "Charlie, is that God?" Charlie looked back at me and chuckled. I could feel Charlie's chuckle in my belly and I could see myself through his eyes.

I knew at that moment that if Charlie and I chose to be together, God/Higher Power would lead us and we would learn how this whole energy — power/empowerment plant — works. I could learn to see myself through Charlie's eyes and, of course, we would both grow because we had Desmond Tutu, aka our combined false self/shadow, waiting back in the room. In summation, in all our hard work and play, we could "develop" the love of our life, which really is *Our Sacred Person* that I described in the last chapter. Our hard work refining our ego/shadow striped the obstructions to being our Soul in relationship to our Higher Self and God.

What does this all mean when our heads are already filled with Hollywood's version of "The Love of Our Life?" It means that no one — no mate — can make us whole or make us feel loved. We do that for our self in relationship with our Higher Power. We "use" our relationships here in this physical reality to help us remove the obstructions to this relationship with our Self and God/Higher Power. This is "True Love." In all truth, I learned that in order to love and be loved, I have to learn/grow to love myself, otherwise I don't have the capacity to know love.

And where does this put my "romance" with Charlie. We are friends, we are partners, we are companions and the most personal part of our relationship will be revealed in the Epilogue of this book called, "Eternal Circle of the Soul."

Authors note: For the Soulful side of natural sex with "The Love of Our Life," see Whitfield B, 1995. *Spiritual Awakenings* Chapter 10, Spiritual Sexuality pages 129-142.

Ж Ж Ж

The Sacred Romance

Brent Curtis and John Eldredge wrote this beautiful explanation in their 1997 book *The Sacred Romance*:

The Sacred Romance calls to us every moment of our lives. It whispers to us on the wind, invites us through the laughter of good friends, reaches out to us through the touch of someone we love. We've heard it in our favorite music, sensed it at the birth of our first child, been drawn to it while watching the shimmer of a sunset on the ocean. It is even present in times of great personal suffering — the illness of a child, the loss of a marriage, the death of a friend. Something calls to us through experiences like these and rouses an inconsolable longing deep within our heart, wakening in us a yearning for intimacy, beauty, and adventure. This longing is the most powerful part of any human personality. It fuels our search for meaning, for wholeness, for a sense of being truly alive. However we may describe this deep desire, it is the most important thing about us, our heart of hearts, the passion of our life. And the voice that calls to us in this place is none other than the voice of God.

Chapter 5

Sharing the Journey as This Life Ends:

The Role of Transition Teams

Making one's transition is so much bigger than any other ritual on this planet. Souls come in. Souls go out. Birth is a joyous event. Death is beyond our comprehension. We live in a material reality that limits our ability to experience the sacred and celebratory side of death: the final passage from this reality to a nonphysical and eternal one.

This nonphysical reality is Spiritual, ineffable and a part of the Divine Mystery. It is the reality of God's world, not our earthly world, and sometimes we can only sense it through our hearts. As the Little Prince said, "It is only with the heart that one can see rightly. What is essential is invisible to the eye." (Saint-Exupéry, 1943)

The enormity and elusiveness of this nonmaterial reality can perhaps only be understood in metaphor. As a respiratory therapist, I used large tanks of oxygen. Each tank contained enough compressed oxygen to make the pressure on the inner walls of the tank 2,200 pounds per square inch. That is an extraordinary amount of pressure. Yet we hooked the tank up to a patient who was receiving the oxygen in a gentle slow stream. The oxygen at the patient's nostrils felt like a soft gentle breeze because of a little device we used called a "reducing valve." Twenty-two hundred pounds per square inch went into the reducing valve, which brought the pressure down to a gentle stream going through the tubing that went to the patient.

As we take in reality, our brains work the same way as the reducing valve. Reality is huge. Its pressure is too big and too much for us to handle. Our brain, our reducing valve, allows reality to flow in a gentle stream so we can handle it without exploding ourselves.

Helping someone die is as close as I can get, as close as any of us can get, to the huge reality that is beyond our individual ability to perceive. Ultimately, all this is a mystery, but we can get closer to the mystery by allowing ourselves to experience death with openness, loss of ego, and willingness to be aware of and open to our subtle experience.

A Beginning Ritual for Ourselves

Each time I have been with a person making his or her transition, I go through my own brief ritual as I travel to be with this person for the first time. I do not plan my ritual. It starts itself with a voice in my head that likes to worry. I hear, "I'm not sure about this one." Or, "How is this going to go?" Or, "I don't know if I'm qualified to do this…this time."

I let myself feel all my insecure feelings and then, instead of worrying, I turn them over. I ask the Universe to help me get my ego out of the way so It may come through. I picture myself as a conduit. I clear by letting everything else in my life move to a back burner where I know it will be safe until I retrieve it. Then I feel prepared to move into someone's final passage in this lifetime.

As I pray, I cross over into another's drama that is filled with possibilities. This final passage can be a healing experience for anyone involved. It can be filled with Spirit and what we call unconditional presence.[8] Over and over again my experiences have shown me that, much of the time, these transition scenes can turn into "Spiritual experiences" that

---

[8]   Welwood 1992

are profound and worthy of any and all human feelings bathed in these sacred moments.

As I walk into the home and am greeted by grieving relatives and friends, I make eye contact with each person who is before me, and I stay present with those who avoid eye contact. As I meet the transitioning person, I focus on my heart and a sense of love. It is as if I am meeting an old friend again. Deep intimacy will usually develop within a very short time because that is our role. This is the reason we, the transition team members, have been asked to come. Our position as part of the team, or as its leader, is to take charge in an unusual way. All the relatives and close significant others in attendance can relax because our presence removes the pressure from them. The transitioning person can relax because there is no more fear of family members and loved ones becoming afraid and calling for an ambulance to take them to a hospital or hospice. They want to die in their own bed. We help them to relax and know that this is now absolutely possible.

And at the same time, we must also let go of ultimate authority over this unpredictable scene and make way for Spirit to orchestrate the transition. We are there to troubleshoot between family members and friends and to gently help with communications. The most important communication will be what the transitioning person wants. We are there to be present, to facilitate and to allow.

The Passing of Time — in No Time

Dying takes its own time. It may become agonizing for everyone involved when it drags on and on. The boring times are rarely spoken about. What started on Friday evening may not conclude until Sunday afternoon or even days beyond. Some relatives may be unwilling to leave or unwilling to take shifts, so there could be a "camp-out" atmosphere that drones on.

I sat for three days with Sherry, a 40-something woman transitioning from cancer (Whitfield, B 1998). It appeared to her that her family was a threat because they wanted her to be in a hospital when she died. My presence not only relieved the pressure from them to move her, it also assured her that she could stay home. Sherry also had unresolved anger over her dead mother's abuse of her as a child. Because of this, she did not want her father, aunts, uncles and cousins to be with her during her transition. As I sat with Sherry, her husband and best friend came in and out, bringing things that were needed, and occasionally to visit. Twice a day the three of us laid our hands on Sherry, said a prayer and meditated with her. This hands-on-healing procedure helped her pain medication to work, gave her a sense of peace and love and gave her husband and friend a chance to share their love with her. No one else was allowed into her room. There were twelve, sometimes fifteen people in the living area of the house who were grieving for Sherry and unable to see her.

The second day of sitting with her, I flipped TV channels at Sherry's request until she said, "Stop!" We were suddenly watching Sally Field screaming over her daughter's grave in *Steel Magnolias*. This scene was so intense, I stayed on my feet, milling around the TV. I found a tape labeled "family" and asked Sherry if we could watch it. What unfolded were Sherry's childhood birthday parties and family vacations. There were her father, aunts, uncles and cousins, showing little Sherry love in the form of hugs and kisses, smiles and admiration. By early that evening, Sherry had invited the entire waiting family into her bedroom.

By late evening, everyone was willing to go home or to other parts of the house to get some sleep. The next afternoon, surrounded by everyone who loved her, Sherry made her transition. It was a process that took about three hours from "coma" to her last breath. During that final day there were tears and deep sadness. But the grieving was also interspersed with stories of wonderful memories. Everyone told stories. As she drifted in and out of consciousness, Sherry smiled and looked around at the faces circling her and her room.

John Loranger

I attended John's death after getting to know him for about six weeks. In his early 30s, he was paralyzed and totally bed-ridden, dependent on the staff to take care of his every need. His only movement came from his ability to speak, and he was quickly losing that too. At the very end he was dependent on an electronic voice box placed on his throat that didn't help the confusion of what he was trying to say.

John fought through his lawyers and friends to be disconnected from life support. This was in the 1980s, and John became the first patient to be allowed to die by being disconnected from life support in Connecticut. I was a witness to that process. When he was disconnected at about 10 am, one of John's last statements through the voice box was, "They are coming for me at 5:30." No one understood what he said, so I repeated his words saying, "He says 'They are coming for me at 5:30.'"

John was given an injection with a sedative and respiratory depressant and went into a peaceful sleep. He was disconnected from the machinery that kept him alive at about 10:10am. But he didn't die right away. He died at exactly 5:30.

The staff showed all the signs of mourning for John because he had been there for several weeks and they all knew and cared for him. But because of this unpredictable way of dying many hours after the life support was removed, and his announcement of when he was to actually die, many staff, including the physicians, acted out in negative ways. Mostly what I heard from them was pain over not being able to control the way John's death happened, and pain over not being able to save his life, plus some unresolved issues that people express when they feel helpless in the face of death.

My Father's Transition

My father collapsed suddenly after a full day's work. We never knew he was chronically ill. My three children and my brother joined me with our mother in south Florida for my father's final day. As I rushed into the hospital unit, a nurse called his doctor, who told me on the phone that my father was in a deep coma and would die soon. I went in and talked to him in his coma, stroking his hair and saying all the things I had not thought I needed to say until that moment. A half hour later, he opened his eyes and talked to me, telling me what I needed to know about taking care of my mother. Then he told me how he wanted to be buried. He fell back to sleep and then awakened a few more times.

When my adult kids came in, he opened his eyes and his face lit up. He adored my kids. "You know what I would love right now?" he said. "A corned beef sandwich." The kids ran to the nearest deli and soon there we were, seven corned beef sandwiches: four of us squeezed around him on his bed and two more standing over him. We reminisced about old times. He gave each one of us a memory that he had obviously held in his heart. Each of us told him how much we loved him and he beamed. And occasionally, my dad, who had never ever talked about the "afterlife" before, spoke to his mother who had died when he was 17. He told us his "Mumma" was there to help him leave. We were held so tightly in that moment that every breath was profound. We knew there was a Presence with us that was part of my father's transition.

Unconditional Presence

When we let go of our ego, love can flow freely. Its bonding effect takes on a kind of atmospheric recognition, akin to humidity but more serene. Then an unconditional presence expands the consciousness of each individual that "brails" what is going on. (Sometimes we can't recognize something in the usual cognitive way so by "brailing" I mean that we feel or sense what is going on around us). I have written several stories concerning this phenomenon (Whitfield Harris B., 1990, Whitfield B 1998).

Every moment is spent in the present, and for those not familiar with this state of unconditional presence, other terms that mean about the same thing are "The Holy Instant" (*A Course In Miracles*), *Be Here Now* (Ram Dass), and Being in the Tao (Eastern mysticism). This concept gives us a whole new way of experiencing our reality. And, it seems that attending the final passage of a loved one, friend or client shows us this heightened sense of reality.

Transpersonal therapist and author John Welwood called this state of consciousness "unconditional presence." He says that when the heart breaks out of its shell, we feel raw and vulnerable. This is the beginning of feeling real compassion for ourselves, because we slow down and authentically see and feel our distress having an impact on us. Then our pain can awaken our desire and will to live in a new way. When we open ourselves to this awareness, it becomes unconditional presence: just being with what is happening in our inner life right now, without any agenda.

That last day with my father, my heart was breaking. At the same time, I was catapulted into this heightened state of awareness. Time had stopped. Every step my feet took registered profoundly. The scenes I viewed in the hospital appeared like virtual reality. Eye contact with another took me directly into that person's being. Each person I connected with knew easily what I was conveying. My connection with my father was total, or more than I had ever realized was possible.[9]

When my father was conscious and with me, he, too, was in this state. Knowing about unconditional presence made it easier for us to "move in" to the situation and take full advantage of it, so that our final moments together, although filled with sadness, could be the best possible.

---

[9] A positive "side effect" of unconditional presence is the realization of the difference between suffering and being in the pain of sadness and grieving. When we suffer, we are resisting what is, and this takes us so deeply into ourselves that we aren't present in the moment. This in turn may cheat us of those possible last precious moments with the transitioning person. Unconditional presence keeps us riveted in the now where there is no resistance. It shows us the difference between suffering and being present with our painful feelings.

Entrainment

Science tells us in the First Law of Thermodynamics that energy doesn't dissipate; it transforms.

When a person gets ready for their transition, as their physical body becomes weaker, their bio-energy weakens. At the same time, their Spiritual energy strengthens. For days or weeks before they leave, they are *transforming*, taking the energy from their physical body and moving it to their Spiritual energy/body. The increasing strength of their Spiritual energy entrains us — the caregivers that are the closest, and sometimes even the next tier out of close people — into the same space. We move into the Spiritual vibration of the dying person.

This process is called "entrainment." Perhaps entrainment is best explained by the example of tuning forks or clocks. When one tuning fork is struck and starts vibrating, other tuning forks nearby will also begin to vibrate. If you have several clocks with pendulums in a room and you start all the pendulums swinging at different times, when you later return to the room, all the pendulums will be swinging in sync.

When we sit in an audience and listen to a compelling speaker, we become entrained. The speaker holds us with their content and delivery. The same thing happens at a musical concert. Then at the end, when we applaud, we break the entrainment and leave as our single self again.

We, the transition team, family members and caregivers may find ourselves entrained during the dying process to the extent that we go through the beginning of the journey with the dying person. Sherry's husband, her best friend and I experienced the Spiritual peace that Sherry was feeling. As her energy became less physical and more Spiritual, the power of her Spirit entrained us. When Sherry's husband and I sat up all night watching her breathe, we soon were breathing in the same pattern she was. We were experiencing entrainment. We were fortunate to experience this state for the entire weekend. Her husband said he continued to experience it for several days after.

Others attending a death often become aware of entrainment, and sometimes even of a Spiritual Presence, moving into the experience of helping someone to let go and transition. We are able to talk about it, to share our feelings and to get a sense of relief for the time being. We know painful grieving may happen afterwards, but for now, there is a strong sense of timelessness and eternity that insulates us from worrying about later grieving. I reassure those that are experiencing this for the first time that this is all right, and I tell them I have written a book that explains this (Whitfield B 1995).

I have received excited phone calls or letters from people after a death, quoting my book on such and such a page, and telling me their experiences. Here is an excerpt from one such letter:

R.E., a 36-year-old medical student:

Another commonality we share is in working with those who are in a human sense 'dying.' Needless to say in my work experience I have been with many people who have passed on. I was the most Spiritually touched however while attending to my mother, my maternal grandparents and my aunt who all left this plane because of terminal illnesses. In attending to them I have had the privilege of experiencing Spiritual connectedness in extraordinary and in what some may call 'mystical' ways. Although humanly painful, these experiences with my family have been a blessing. I too come from a severely dysfunctional family and it wasn't unfortunately until I was grown and my family members were ill that I realized how much they loved me. Spirit helped me to understand that all of the conflict was necessary for all of us to grow at our own rate and according to our own Spiritual readiness."

Humility at Work

When lecturing to hospice volunteers and staff over the years, I marvel at the people I meet. They are so aware. They are fun-loving and full of "high energy." They love what they are doing and they love the camaraderie they share. They are also aware of burnout and pace themselves because of it. They have taught me much! My dying patients have taught me even more. I have learned so much about the wonderful possibilities we share. And it seems that the best time to share and blossom in our human/divine nature is during the transition of a Soul back to Spirit.

There are humbling moments during this process that help us to absolutely know that our lives and our transitions are orchestrated by something higher. These moments are termed "synchronicities." Synchronicities are linking coincidences that happen often enough to make us realize that our lives are woven from an elevated awareness. Synchronicities usually punctuate Spirit's presence and, even in the saddest moments, may transform grief to a fleeting sense of joy. Ordinary things take on special meanings i.e.: a piece of wax falling from a candle is transformed into the shape of an angel, songs on the radio are giving messages about the very thing we were just thinking or speaking of, phone calls start coming from people we were just talking about. (See chapter 10 on page 121 for more on synchronicity).

Death, the Final Celebration In This Lifetime

Souls come in and Souls go out. Birth is a time of celebration. Final Passages can be too. Many Souls I have worked with know/believe that they will soon recover — on the other side of the veil. They may be weary of the dying process and prefer to leave to start their recovery. They may be "hanging on" only because their close others are not ready to let them go. This is where we can do our part in helping them in their transition. We can work with the others to help them realize that the most loving thing we can do is to let go and give our loved ones permission to leave. It has been suggested that each Soul waits for permission from another to transition. I have seen it work that way.

A gentle way to do this is to give the transitioning person a foot massage. They need to be touched. Hand massages work too but I always go for the feet. I can stand at the foot of the bed, rubbing their feet, and even if their eyes are closed, many times they open and gaze into mine. If I am the person that is going to give them permission to leave, I will gently say, "It's all right. If you need to go now, you go." Of course, if this is a loved one, I will tell them I love them too, but if they're ready it's all right to go now. I kept reassuring my father that we would take care of our mother, and he looked relieved. I could feel his relief.

After they transition, the sense of a profound Spiritual experience may continue for a while, for at least as long as the others stay together. That is why it is so hard to leave and go back to our own lives. The "Wake," or the Jewish tradition of "Sitting Shiva," helps in this regard. We spend more time grieving and finding comfort with others. Eventually, though, we must all go back to our individual lives, and then the sense of being in a Spiritual experience disappears. Reading about Spiritual experiences may help.

Paul's Story

Paul Furgalack was a computer service technician for 15 years. He came to see me twice to discuss his grandmother and the possibility of taking me to visit her. She was 97, blind and in a nursing home. His uncle had told him and the rest of the family not to visit her. Their uncle had told Paul she didn't want anyone to see her in this condition.

Most of what we discussed in the first two visits was about what Paul wanted to happen. He believed that I, or we, could help her to understand that it was all right to leave. And he missed her and wanted to see her before she died.

We went to the nursing home after visiting hours to make sure we wouldn't meet with his uncle. Before we went in, we joined hands and prayed in the parking lot. I told him in advance about hands-on healing work, and I stood by as he touched and loved his 97-year-old grandmother. I explain this hands-on healing meditation below.

Paul told me later, "I felt a oneness with us outside in the prayer circle. I felt a oneness with us and my grandmother even thought she wasn't out there with us. And, I felt a oneness with the sky. It felt good and it brought tears to my eyes. I didn't know then that I was in the beginning of a Spiritual experience.

"It felt like we were being sly, sort of sneaking in after visiting hours. You made a connection with my grandmother right away and that felt so good because I really wanted that to happen. After that it was something more. I felt something I could grasp but couldn't understand.

Paul continued, "After that, when we stopped for dessert, you mentioned massage school and then you sent me a catalogue from there. Just an hour earlier — touching my grandmother — I knew I had to go back to school for massage therapy. And now the people I help, help me to understand that when you help someone through touch, 'It' is Spiritual. This is the real education of the Spiritual path. I wanted to help my grandmother. I wanted to get her connected up. And I got connected up and it totally changed my life. What happened in the parking lot was profound and it changed my life. I now know — I am a child of God and I probably have God in every cell in my body. I think that this is the way God works — through all of us."

A few years later Paul wrote me and said:

"My father died on Father's Day, June of '96....He suffered for almost a year. I touched and massaged my dad every chance I had. We all had hopes that he would rally from it but no chance....Because of what I had learned from you, I whispered into my dad's ear, 'Dad, I want you to know that I love you and that you have been a loving and caring father to all of your sons. You have been suffering too long; no one should ever suffer the way you have been....I need to tell you that it's OK to let go of this life and meet up with your mom, dad, brother and sister....If permission is what you need to let go, then, out of my love for you I am granting you all the permission you need to let go and when my time comes I will meet you there.' He must have known that all of his sons would be coming to see him on Father's Day, which they did and at 11:30pm that night he died. This is the son of the grandmother you met."

Hands-on Healing Meditation

This type of hands-on energy work is easy to use with people making their transition. The one receiving the energy lies down and is usually covered with a light blanket. Other members of the family, friends or health care team (whom the receiver feels are "safe") gather around and sit with their hands gently and lightly touching the receiver. Before we begin, I always say a prayer to connect and unite us all in what we are asking to do. I say something like, "Dear God (or Dear Holy Mother, or whatever my patient feels most comfortable with), please may we be instruments of your healing energy and your Oneness. Please help us to get our egos out of the way so You may come through."

This works with one person as an instrument, or as many as six. The main principle is that the people that are doing the hands-on-healing feel safe to the patient receiving the energy. I have worked with children as young as three in a healing circle, and adults as old as 90 who may be dying themselves. In one such case, when we had finished the first healing, we covered that patient, and then a 90-year-old laid down on the floor a few feet away, and we repeated the healing on her. Then something extraordinary happened. One of the people helping with these two hands-on healings was an eight-year-old girl who was also in the family. She was suffering from repeated stomach aches and asked if she could be helped. We then did a healing on her. Her mother called me a few weeks later to tell me that she was going through a painful divorce and since it had started, her little girl had stomach pain to the point where they had taken her to a medical specialist for tests. The tests were normal. And, since we did the healings that day her daughter has been pain free. This mother was in school to become an acupuncturist and after experiencing that day with the healings she now believed more than ever in energy work.

It doesn't matter if the people giving the healing believe in all this. All that matters is that they have the intention of wanting to help. Many times the person receiving healing tells me afterwards that their pain medication is now working or they no longer feel they need it. Their coloring improves, they feel more relaxed and they feel loved.

Hands-on-healing can be done twice a day, or more, if the patient requests it. The givers have often told me that they calmed down from the experience. It not only helped their bodies to relax, it also helped their hearts to know that they were giving "something" to the person in need. This is especially important for loved ones who may have been afraid to touch the patient for fear of hurting them. This gives them a safe way to express themselves that bypasses words.

Whether the patient is going to get better or is going to die doesn't matter in these hands-on circles. We are not looking for a "cure." We are looking for a sharing that brings comfort to the receiver, and usually spills over into the givers.

We do this together for about 20 minutes. It feels like a meditation. We clear our minds and sit in a peaceful way, placing our hands gently on the patient and sharing a current of Energy that envelops all of us. We naturally come out of it within 20 minutes or so, feeling more relaxed and at the same time energized, because the energy we shared didn't come from us but through us.

We close this healing circle with a prayer of gratitude: "Dear God, Dear Spirit, thank you for allowing us to be instruments of your healing Energy. Thank you for allowing us to feel your Oneness. Amen"

Support Groups for Grieving

After an all-night vigil, I sometimes feel I have "shrunk" inside to "make room" for the dying person. It's a feeling of almost losing one's self. I am able to leave and go home, take a soothing bath and relax in my own bed.

Many times, the primary caregiver is sharing their bed with the person we have been helping to transition. The primary caregiver has no place to go to get themselves back. The close or primary caregiver, who is often the significant other, and who is living, painfully, through this process of escalating illness and dying, is living this loss 24 hours a day. Counseling primary caregivers during their loved one's transition and after it is over contains this common thread of loss of self as well as loss of the other.

Often primary caregivers are afraid to complain for fear of feeling self-ish or guilty for a number of reasons that only continue to damage them inside. Of course, they want to be everything they can be to their dying loved ones. But we are all still human, and we all still have needs. We can gently help them to remember that they, too, are losing a partner, or parent, or friend, so part of them is dying also. One of the best things we can do to assist them is to help make a plan to leave for a while when they can, even if it is only to take a walk or to sit in a park.

I have often been a speaker for a group called "Compassionate Friends." This group is for parents who have lost children. Some members have lost a child only a month earlier; others may have been attending this group for 20 years. You might want to find out if a similar group is available in your area so that you can refer your friend or client's families. Self-care is important. Let the caregivers know this. There are local support groups for caregivers in every large city and even in small towns. Local cancer societies are a good source for finding them. If caregivers cannot leave home, help them to find a support group online.

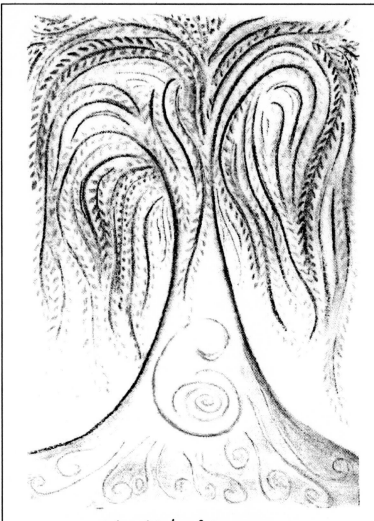

It is with joyful sorrow
that we announce both the
birth and passing of our
beloved son, Noah

Chapter 6

Why do Children Die?

I am a public speaker. I don't just speak for myself but for the thousands of Near-Death Experiencers who my colleagues and I have interviewed. I believe I am also a voice for the people I have sat with as they have transitioned.

I have given talks in churches, hospitals, hospices, universities, and conferences for nurses and medical staffs. Occasionally someone from an audience will ask me to explain how God could let children or young people die. I am at a loss because I can't explain why children die. However, I can and do tell the stories of the children I have been with as they were dying, and they comforted us.

Willie, a five-year-old who I visited in a Ronald McDonald House actually forced his mother to open up and talk with me by jumping up into her lap and forcing her crossed arms open. Then he placed his little hands on her cheeks and squeezed until her mouth opened. At that moment she finally cried after holding in her feelings for too long. Then he jumped down and continued to run around the room and play like any five-year-old.[10] I counseled this mom for about an hour and a half and before I left, the little boy put his hands on my temples and stared

---

[10] This story in more detail is told in my first book *Full Circle* (Harris B & Bascom L, Simon and Schuster Pocket Books, 1990) . See chapter about Willie.

into my eyes. He let me know, without words, but heart to heart, that he was all right and for the rest of that day I experienced a spiritual level of consciousness that can only be explained through entrainment. His little hands and those beautiful eyes took me to where he was. He might have been dying of cancer but he showed me how he was experiencing this reality. It was ineffable and peaceful at the same time.

Noah

Not long ago, our daughter Kate sent me these emails she has been writing with Chris, a childhood friend. They live across the country from each other now so emails bridge the gap. Chris and his wife, Jen had just lost a child at birth. Kate describes herself as being Spiritual in the same way Charlie and I are. Chris is a self-professed agnostic. Perhaps their dialogue can begin to open us up to finding our own Soul's answers. (Note: the emails below are unedited, just as they were sent).

To: Chris Lyons

From: Kate Hart

Good Mornin' Chris.

How are you doing today?

How is Jen and how are the boys?

To: Kate Hart

From: Chris Lyons

Very sad Kate. Today was Noah's due date. This is the most horrible feeling I have ever experienced.

To: Chris Lyons

Subject: RE: mornin

Dear Chris

I remembered this was your day. I wish I could make every-thing be okay again. Now I look at Anna and wonder what life would be like without her and I just don't know how sad you must be. Maybe it would be sadder to watch a sick child being sick. Maybe Noah was blessed to not be living out a sick life. It still doesn't make things better, I realize. During the pregnancy was Jen feeling pretty connected with the baby's movements and you guys feeling like you already "knew" him? Or was it different? Does Jen have mixed feelings about inducing early, or was that the only option? It would have been harder to wait out another month, I'd think. Was this all happening so fast that it seems like a blur?

The one time I ever felt like I was losing my mind was after I found out that my boyfriend was lying to me, and my whole life was not what I thought it to be. I remember lying on a mattress crying and crying, and whatever I tried to do, I just couldn't get my mind to rest and stop thinking about everything. It was so overwhelming I could not sleep or do anything else. The only thing that saved me was having an extremely shy stray cat named Yoda in the room with me, constantly meowing and wanting me to pet it non-stop for hours and hours. I think she could recognize that I was not a threat to her, and each meow brought my mind back to the present, away from my problem. I don't know why I told you that, I guess it's one of the worst feelings I've felt. It was just such a bad feeling to have my mind always thinking about it. I just needed a break for my mind, it was so drain-ing.

Maybe this is not the time for babies on earth. Maybe their pure Souls are needed to soothe other Souls before they can return to earth.

Could the world need us to learn more lessons about how precious life is? The world does need more compassion. But at what price? And from who? The ones who were already compassionate?

How is Jen?

To: Kate Hart

From: Chris Lyons

Kate,

We couldn't really wait as Noah's abdomen would have been so swollen that a vaginal birth would have not been likely. It was very important to give him the birth he deserved. I hope I have not freaked you out. Jen and I had a bad night last night, so we got drunk. Neither one of us ever drink so it was quite effective, she is doing about as well as anyone could.

To: Chris Lyons

From: Kate Hart

Dear Chris,

So, what did you have? Beer? Or some of the harder stuff? I prefer red wine, myself, although we do not drink either.

I like how you said "give him the birth he deserved." Very admirable. So, as Jen was in labor, did you know if the baby would even survive at all? What did they tell you? (How much did they know?)

To: Kate Hart

From: Chris Lyons

Kate,

Wine for Jen. Vodka for me.

We knew we had a 50/50 chance for Noah to survive birth.

To: Chris Lyons

From: Kate Hart

Dear Chris,

Did Noah have more of a chance to survive after birth, or did you know it was only going to be a short time? Did you choose cremation? Will there be a site you can visit? These are hard questions for me to ask.

I am glad your folks are there for you. They are very sweet people, always took the time to make me feel special. I still buy those chocolate-covered cherries every year and think of them.

To: Kate Hart

From: Chris Lyons

Kate,

We knew he had zero chance of survival. He was cremated and we are having a local potter make his urn. You should be getting his announcement in the mail shortly.

He looked like any other newborn, he just did not have any kidneys and very underdeveloped lungs.

To: Chris Lyons

From: Kate Hart

Chris, Was he beautiful?

To: Kate Hart

From: Chris Lyons

Absolutely! His picture is on the announcement. The boys are really upset about losing their brother.

To: Chris Lyons

From: Kate Hart

Oh, Chris, that sounds like such a beautiful way to celebrate him. Very well done.

How did you spend that hour? Gazing at him and loving him, I'd imagine.

Did the boys get to meet him? From what my boss said about her sister's family, Ian may not remember much but Graham will be affected more. What have they said about it? Are they worried that something bad will happen to them? What do you tell a child about death when you don't believe in God?

To: Kate Hart

From: Chris Lyons

Boys did not meet him. Ian too young and g said he did not want to, it would make him too sad. They both talk about

Noah almost daily and tell people about their brother that died. No mention of their fate. Told the boys Noah was an angel baby, G said but "no one <u>really</u> knows if heaven is real" and I agreed. Ian said he didn't want an angel baby. He wanted to reach up and grab his wings and have a walking baby. What do you tell a child about death when you believe in god? What is god, anyway?

To: Chris Lyons

From: Kate Hart

Dear Chris,

I like what you said about the angel baby. I like what the boys said too.

When our kitty had to be put to sleep, I told Nicholas that his body was hurting and almost finished, and that because of that we would have to say good bye to him for now, but that we could see him again one day when we were all with God. I told him that kitty's Soul was leaving his body; that while the body that he needed here on earth was finished living, the cat inside — the Soul — would continue to live on, but in a different form that we cannot see. Somehow Nick placed all his faith in that belief immediately and was able to feel like kitty's life didn't just end, that there may be a chance for us to reconnect with this Soul in the future.

I didn't know if I was telling Nicholas the truth because "who knows really." I had thoughts of him feeling duped or being angry at me to find out the truth, but if we really do just turn to dust — Souls and all — then we will *really never know the difference*. For some, knowing the truth is what's most important. For others, it's more important to have something (pleasant) to believe in, something to soothe the Soul. If the truth cannot be determined from here, then who are we to doubt anyone's beliefs in the first place? Maybe it's just my perspective, but I like to think there is some level of "understood faith." It's like we all kind of understand that no one really knows what happens when you die, but are all sharing in the hope and faith that when we die we will return to a loving and familiar place, hopefully connecting with that higher power that gives us peace. In doing so (having faith), we can find comfort for ourselves.

To ask for something to believe in is human nature. Anything we can't see with our eyes is hard to believe. We ask our parents, our clergy, our society, our God and ourselves if there really is a God. Some would say no, that if God is all loving, he/she could not possibly let tragedies occur here on Earth, and how can all of that be explained? I believe that we are born into a world of opposites, and that we have to have one to have the other, light and dark, life and death, etc. I do not think God is in control of everything we do, but is more of an existence of love, who just kind of hangs out as a source of comfort for us all. God = Good.

I think it's all about the inner Soul and connecting to a higher power in our quest for peace. It's also about learning and growing. That explains why we are here on earth — to learn particular lessons that might help us reach that peace we're so desperately searching for.

I also believe in reincarnation. I believe that the same Souls come back to be with each other again and again here on earth, to learn from our experiences and those of others. I believe that the Souls have a choice in the earth lesson they choose. I do not know how to explain your situation.

It sounds like it may be one of your and Jen's core issues that you came to earth to learn about, with Noah being your teacher. Maybe if that is the case, you can try to determine what it is you are learning, and become more aware of it and why it might help you to find your own peace. Maybe think of what it was that Noah wanted you to know...ok, see, his name is "Noah," after all. Also think of what he came to represent to you. Just what exactly did he come here to say and do? If you can find a life purpose for him, regardless of the length of his life, maybe you can find peace in the idea that he really did come here to do just what he did, and that it must have worked on some level. Maybe this time his life was more about you and Jen than it was about him. That sounds like a really special Soul. You are lucky to have been chosen. Now what could he be telling us....?

Someday, When Anna asks about God, I will tell her the same thing I told her brother, because I like what I see in Nicholas's faith. Sometimes a child just needs something (or someone) to believe in. Sometimes we all do. When I saw the relief in Nick's eyes to know that none of us really ever go away for good, it was quite possibly more of a comfort to me than it was to him!

I think whatever you tell the boys is going to be right for them, you are their father. They will come to you first for their faith. They will request and expect answers so that they might soothe their own Souls. If you find that you have a child who is looking to believe in something, you might offer him different perspectives or ideas about life continuing on some level, which it sounds like you are doing. Somehow, until we really need God, God is not always at the front of our minds. Maybe Noah is bringing you God. Ok, this is getting weird now, why did you choose the name again? Or did it just come to you? What does the name Noah mean to *you*?

Kate

To: Kate Hart

From: Chris Lyons

Dear Kate,

Wow. Very eloquent.

Sounds like you and Jen have a lot in common on this subject. I'm the agnostic not Jen. I appreciate your words and obvious concern, it means more to me than I can say.

Maybe one day I will find "faith" I REALLY would like to, but as I have said before it just ain't there for me. As you touched on, we as mere mortals/humans want so desperately to have a definite explanation for existence and thereafter…BUT … I don't think we have the capacity to explain the unexplainable...

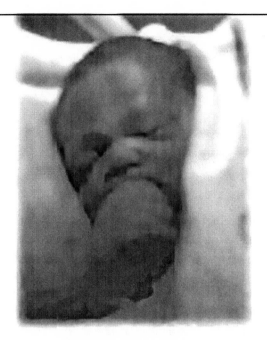

Noah Raynham Lyons
December 29, 2004

Dear Friends and Family,

We share this news with you, not to sadden you, but to let you know that during Noah's short time spent with us, he knew no suffering, only the love and warmth that surrounded him. Noah made a profoundly deep impact on our lives. As such, we want his life to be celebrated and his name to be spoken. While it might make us cry, it will also bring us great joy.
He will live in our hearts forever.
With Peace & Love,

Chris and Jen Lyons

Author's note: I chose to share the account of Noah and his family because it may offer you, the reader, a successful path to your Soul. It certainly did to mine. I sobbed and felt Chris and Jen's pain over and over as I read this chapter. Still, I probably did not feel a fraction of what they felt. But I still felt it. Who couldn't feel it? A child dying right after it is born is so unbelievably painful. But the real impact here comes from the way Noah's parents, Chris and Jen, opened their Souls to him. They didn't try to protect themselves by treating this birth and tragedy as a "clinical situation." They could have. The medical community has offered that response for decades.

Noah's body may not have been able to sustain life here, but because Chris and Jen's love protected Noah's Soul, we may even dare to hope that he chooses to come in again. And, they allowed themselves to grieve, to feel the pain as it came up for them. This is another way they honored their child.

Chris and Jen gave him the love, respect and the reverence that his brief visit here in this physical reality warranted. Although Chris questions his "faith" and isn't sure whether he believes in anything at all, I believe that his and Jen's response are among the most courageous and Spiritual calls human beings can extend to one another.

Jen and Chris's integrity through this loss demonstrated a kind of reverence for life that comes from love and wholeness — the kind of love and wholeness that some call "God" or "God-like." I believe that Chris and Jen showed us how they, and we, can be a reflection of a Higher Power that is a Divine Mystery and at the same time a Mystery we can call upon in our deepest pain and our happiest moments.

For Chris, the God of his understanding did not come down from "above." I believe that Chris's God came from within Chris and Jen and through them. Their choices during Noah's birth and transition back to God are a constant reminder to us of how sacred and loving life is when we navigate from the deepest part of our being. "Believing" in God is all about words. Their love and joy toward Noah and from him are the *action*, the earthly reality of what we choose to call God.

Letter to Rachel's Parents

By **Ram Dass**

A number of years ago the Spiritual teacher Ram Dass responded to the distraught parents of a child who had just died in a tragic murder. His response in the following letter in many ways is similar to and expands what we identified in our own response to Noah's story, (as well as what I discuss in the next chapter on grieving such a loss).

> Dear Steve and Anita,
>
> Rachel finished her work on earth, and left the stage in a manner that leaves those of us left behind with a cry of agony in our hearts, as the fragile thread of our faith is dealt with so violently. Is anyone strong enough to stay conscious through such teaching as you are receiving? Probably very few. And even they would only have a whisper of equanimity and peace amidst the screaming trumpets of their rage, grief, horror and desolation.
>
> I can't assuage your pain with any words, nor should I. For your pain is Rachel's legacy to you. Not that she or I would inflict such pain by choice, but there it is. And it must burn its purifying way to completion. For something in you dies when you bear the unbearable, and it is only in that dark night of the Soul that you are prepared to see as God sees, and to love as God loves.
>
> Now is the time to let your grief find expression. No false strength. Now is the time to sit quietly and speak

to Rachel, and thank her for being with you these few years, and encourage her to go on with whatever her work is, knowing that you will grow in compassion and wisdom from this experience.

In my heart, I know that you and she will meet again and again, and recognize the many ways in which you have known each other. And when you meet you will know, in a flash, what now it is not given to you to know: Why this had to be the way it was.

Our rational minds can never understand what has happened, but our hearts — if we can keep them open to God — will find their own intuitive way. Rachel came through you to do her work on earth, which includes her manner of death. Now her Soul is free, and the love that you can share with her is invulnerable to the winds of changing time and space. In that deep love, include me.

In love,

Ram Dass

Author's note:. Grateful acknowledgement to Ram Dass for permission to reprint the above letter.

You may find this letter at www.ramdasstapes.org/articles_final.htm.

Chapter 7

Grieving

Good Grief
Stop the World
I need to get off.
Feeling a squeeze
Somewhere in my being.

Stop the world!
And my monkey brain
Chatter!
For all that was
And never will be.

Stop my head
And this thing called
"Logic."
Get to the right
And "Braille"
This whole thing.

Give up some smiles
And the stress behind
Them.

Barbara Harris Whitfield

Alleviate Grief
By jumping in
And being it.
BHW

Sooner or later we all need to grieve. It is a slow, difficult, and emotionally painful process. Whether we are the one leaving or the one letting go of someone we love, grieving is the same.

If we are open and willing — there is always a "gift." My personal experience of grieving is that it usually reveals more of our Soul — for both
my own losses and those people I have helped. Who (or whatever) we
have lost activates more of our heart, more of our ability to love our
self and life. However, this takes humility and patience, as described in
The Power of Humility. Humility in this context is the openness and willingness to learn more about our Self, others and the God of our
Understanding.

Elizabeth Kubler-Ross (1997) suggests that when we are faced with our
own death, or the death of a loved one, we experience five emotional
stages. The first stage is *denial*. This usually occurs when we are first
informed that we will die soon. In the beginning, we are in shock and
are unable to accept this fact. The second stage is *anger*. At this stage
we blame others for our death, and we envy others who are able to
live longer than us. The third stage is *bargaining*. During this stage, we try
to negotiate with others who might have some control over our fate,
such as doctors, angels and divine beings, in order to prolong our lives.
This is usually unsuccessful and we end up in the fourth stage, *depression*. In the earlier parts of this stage we lose hope and begin feeling as
if there is nothing we can do to avoid our destiny. Soon, this depression
will move into a preparatory stage where we focus primarily on the fact
that we will not be able to enjoy the company of our loved ones after
we die. Lastly, we complete the process of letting go of our desire to
live longer and enter the *acceptance* stage. In this stage, we are calm and

peaceful and learn to appreciate the remaining moments we have left in this lifetime (Sato, T 2003).

In my experiences helping people prepare for their transition, I have found that they often skip many of the above stages and move into acceptance because 1) they are naturally Spiritual in their belief that they will awaken in another reality, and 2) they have been in so much pain they are ready to drop this body and look forward to recovering on the other side.

Learning what is real

I've learned much from my patients, relatives, and friends whom I have been with during the dying process. The poem below by Chris H. Norman will illustrate this. Chris was diagnosed with Amyotrophic lateral sclerosis (ALS) the day before his 50th birthday. While ALS is a terminal physical disease, for Chris it has also become a Spiritual journey. He writes: "Spiritually, I have never been happier as this has become a journey of love. The dreams of the last six months have been so profound and have bordered on the mystical. They continue to affirm the absolute beauty of this path, for me as well as this growing web of family and friends. By going through this transition with love and gratitude, we all grow and become larger."

What I Have Learned

By

Chris H. Norman

I have learned that the most important things in life are the ones done with love.

I have learned that playing and laughing are some of the healthiest things we can do.

I have learned that we live in a world full of miracles: the love we have for our mates and friends, the birth of our children, and the sounds of laughter are all miracles.

I have learned that it is impossible to be grateful and not be happy.

I have learned that an individual who has cultivated forgiveness has a sense of peace.

I have learned that emotions only have the strength we allow. This is especially true of fear, worry, anger, and jealousy.

I have learned that there is a natural rhythm to the universe. The sun rises. The sun sets. Tides sweep in. Tides sweep out. Nothing stands still. Everything flows to a natural order.

I have learned that life is a continuous, rhythmic experience of mistakes and successes, adding to knowledge and expression.

I have learned that what we learn is for eternity, as we are forever beings.

I have learned that life is a journey towards inheritance.

I have learned that each flower, each blade of grass, each sunrise and sunset, each snowflake is absolutely unique. There has never been a better you, and there never, ever will be.

I have learned that we have the support of the Universe, whether we acknowledge it or not.

I have learned that our minds are part of the mind of God. Our hearts are part of the Heart of God. We eventually return to God and our thoughts will share the thoughts of all creation and our heart will beat with the heart of God.

I have learned that we are God's agent with our hearts faintly echoing His song.

We are to make ourselves a part of that song, so those who have lost the tune may remember it again.

I have learned to rest and let Him hold me.

When you reach out, touch His hand and then put your arm around a friend.

The most important things in life are the ones done with love...

$$\text{X} \quad \text{X} \quad \text{X}$$

Our relationship with grieving

As someone transitions, their physical energy weakens and transforms into stronger Spiritual energy; I have been privileged to witness and experience that process. This is why I wrote about entrainment (see page 58). If there is a natural setting where loved ones can relax with the dying person and the process can take over, we are transformed by this energy during those final moments, and perhaps for the rest of our lives. This helps the people who are left behind to not only grieve more easily, but also to know there is something bigger going on. As you will read below, in Carole's Story, a few months after her transition, I experienced her communicating with me. Others have had similar experiences to mine, so we are left with a sense that our lost loved one continues on, not only on the other side of the veil, but also as though they are still with us in our hearts or energy fields.

I have met and studied with Elizabeth Kubler-Ross. Her stages were and are a good beginning foundation for learning about our relationship with grieving and our relationship with someone who is dying, including ourselves. My experiences, however, have led me to take a step further. I have learned that the best way to help is to stand back and be a witness, to validate the feelings, problems, pain, needs and wants of the dying person and to negotiate what they need with the other grieving people nearby. I also suggest removing the order of the stages Elizabeth talked and wrote about. We don't do the grieving process; it does us. If we can let go of always needing to control and let things come up naturally on their own, half the battle will be over. Grieving teaches us how to be natural and let go into the flow of life in a new way, including our inner life.

The most overwhelming lesson that I learned in doing my own grieving process is that *there are feelings within me that are stronger than my will to control them.* I had to give in and let them move and do at their own pace.

I asked Charlie about grieving and he said, "Elizabeth's original 'stages' of grieving have been explored by many. It seems that her original structure was somewhat stereotyped and rigid. While she described the basic nuts and bolts of grieving, it turns out that grieving is a much more diverse and fluid process regarding experience, especially time. There is no specific time limit that grieving takes. Key in the process is having 'safe others' around us as we grieve. People who try to intervene with their own agendas on our personal process can actually slow or even block our ability to grieve."

Don't just do something ... stand there.

Many years ago, Charlie studied with a nun, Sister Chaminode, who was teaching the way she had learned to work with dying people. Sister Chaminode was able to sum up her experiences in one easy sentence taken from the old adage, "Don't just stand there... do something!" She reversed it to demonstrate that when we are assisting in the dying process, the best we can do is... *nothing!* Just stand there. Just *be* with the person — just witness and validate their feelings, their intuitions, and their truths. Stand there with love in our hearts and help them to embrace their true identity.

Depression Vs. Sadness

There's a big difference between being depressed and being sad. When we grieve, sadness overtakes us and rules our life for quite a while. But there is movement. Eventually we move through sadness and make meaning out of our loss. When I am depressed, I am numb and there is no movement or stuck grief. Our societies used to make room for the grieving process. We had periods of time where we were supported on many levels by our group. Now, grieving has been reduced to a few days off work and then back to business as usual. Rather than honor healthy grieving, our society, as exemplified by drug companies, has convinced us that we are depressed and that drugs will relieve our pain. Prescription drugs only put our grief work on "hold" where it will remain until we stop the drugs and let go into feeling the pain. It takes courage to face our loss, but from that process can come new ways of being that are our gift from the one who transitioned.

Shame or Low Self-Esteem

Another thing I've learned from helping people grieve and my own grief process is that while we are in the thick of it, our self esteem drops. Another word for low self-esteem is *shame*. This is an inevitable part of grieving. In contrast to *guilt*, which makes us feel bad for *doing* something wrong, we feel shame for *being* something wrong or bad. Thus guilt seems to be correctable or forgivable, whereas there seems to be no way out of shame.

Shame is universal to being human. If we do not work through it and then let go of it, shame tends to accumulate and burden us more and more, until we even become its victim.

Talking about our shame or low self-esteem to safe others is a way to alleviate it. Support groups are also a safe place to express this type of pain. Be aware that, as long as we are in the grieving process, we will have an underlying sense of low self-esteem. It's a part of grieving that seems to stick around until the end of the process.

My experience and the experience of others I have helped most often shows an increase in self-esteem when we have completed our grief work. We don't return to the same life because we are not the same person as when we started. Life is different because we are different. There are sometimes hidden gifts we receive in our life from the loss of a loved one.

Grieving for My Parents

Getting through the sadness of losing a loved one takes time, years. When I lost my dad, I had waves of sadness that would flow over me and take me, and then numbness set in between. The numbing served to help me take care of necessary chores. Then another wave of sadness washed over me and I sat with it. In the beginning, after the initial several days of numbness during the period of the memorial service and burial, the cycles of sadness and numbness occurred four or more times a day. After a few months, the cycles continued 3 times a day. And so on until, after a year, the cycle happened about once a day.

Over the years, I have come to feel my father in my heart. All that he was to me in a positive way is carried in my memories and actually creates a warm feeling in my heart. All that he was to me in a negative or painful way I continued to work on during the grieving period. Our relationship continued during that process and the painful memories have dropped away now, leaving me continuously with that warm feeling that I carry in my heart.

My mother died on a Tuesday in a hospital near her home in South Florida in 1994. Her body functions had been deteriorating for years. I got the call as Charlie and I were checking in to a hotel in Seattle,

Washington for an American Holistic Medical Association Convention. He was speaking on Wednesday. I was to talk on Saturday, the last day of the convention.

I was on the first plane headed for Florida early Wednesday morning. I thought about all the people I had helped die with honesty and openness, in contrast to how I could never talk about anything real with my mother. We never talked about her death. I could never be myself with her. Tears came and I started to grieve.

I talked to God during the seven-hour flight to Florida. I knew from my NDE that God doesn't judge. I know from that experience that we are all God's children, including my mother. But somehow I had to explain to God my parents' plight in this lifetime. They had terrible trauma in their childhoods. They suffered extreme pain. I asked for them to feel my love. I prayed for their release and for my brother and me to be able to grieve and go on living.

The next day we buried our mother next to our father. We stayed for two days trying to sit shiva in between taking care of everything we had to do.

I flew back to Seattle for the last day of the conference. My talk was the first one in the morning, and I heard myself telling 400 physicians and healthcare providers that my mother had just died. I told them about the physician who had waited for my daughter and then prayed over my mother as he unplugged her from the ventilator. I knew his kindness was now being "caught" by 400 more doctors and nurses. I heard myself say I felt hope for my mother now that she was released and was with God. Then I gave my talk on "Death, Dying and the Near-Death Experience." I received an unexpected and long standing ovation.

Flying home from Seattle to Baltimore, I started grieving for myself. Both my parents were gone. I had never had a childhood. Once I grew up, I spent years healing. My NDE showed me that trying to heal was much better than numbing out or turning around and becoming an abuser myself.

After each of my parents died, I went around and around feeling my pain, letting it go and feeling it again. Grieving is a strange state. It is a process that took hold of me and ran my life. I continued to work. The rest of my time was dictated to me by the grieving process. I realized after a while that I couldn't hurt so much for very long. I would cry intensely for about 15 minutes, and then stop. Then I could numb out for a while or process a memory.

One night, about nine months after my mother died, and almost two years after my dad's death, I was in bed ready to fall asleep. Perhaps I was already asleep, but it felt as if I was awake and looking into the dark, and the darkness was like another dimension:

My father was lying down to my upper left. My mother wandered in from the right, as her True Self, her Soul. "Where am I?" she asks.

"You have died," I reply.

"Oh. Where's Daddy?"

He died, too," I answer. "He's over there."

My mother wanders over to him and puts her arm around his torso and helps him up.

"What are we supposed to do?" she asks.

I answer, "You can go to be with God now."

"We don't know how."

"Follow my prayers." And I pray with all my heart for God to receive my parents.

My parents float away. They are moving with my prayers. And as they do, a terrible stabbing pain, like that of a knife wound, comes out of my back at heart level, as if grazing my scapula, and then disappears. I know a part of

*me has gone with them. I know they are with God. I feel at peace, and I am
happy for them.*

There was something so different about my mother in this dream.
Because it was more real than any dream I had ever had, I questioned
whether it was a dream, or something more. Similar to my NDE, it had
an "other-worldly" sense to me. I believe that I was in contact with both
my parents' Souls and that they were confused, as many Souls are after
they die. It's not over for them, or us, after we "die." We continue on
our journey of exploration and growth.   The only word I can come up
with to explain the way my mother came across to me in this experience is "disarmed." All of her wounding and her defensiveness from this
lifetime had dropped away, and I was clearly seeing her Soul, exhausted
but clearly her *authentic* self.

My grieving process has lightened up since that dream. I sense that most
of my pain over my parents' deaths is over. Occasionally I still grieve for
them, for me and for what we missed.

Writing the above, I grieved some more. And through all of this grief
work I have learned to let go of trying to control this process. Like my
mother in my dream, I am disarmed. I have no defensiveness left against
feeling my feelings. I have experientially learned from the loss of my
father and mother that we can't control grieving. It is like having a
chronic disease. It comes and it goes. But when it flares up, watch out.
Listen to it, to its needs. We need to stop doing and just be with it. The
more we struggle against it or try to ignore it, the greater the flare-up
becomes. This process of grief is a caving in and a letting go and a breaking through to feelings.

Over time I had put a shell around certain feelings; then the feelings had
hardened and become more difficult to work through and release. Now
when a feeling comes up, if I can just sit and be with it — let it express
itself through my body or my mood — it will eventually transform.
Sometimes it becomes tears that dissolve away tension within my body,

my mind or my Soul. Sometimes the feeling transforms into an insight or revelation. Sometimes it is unintelligible, and if I can just be with it, it will go away.

What am I learning? Mountains of stuff. I needed to grieve for being my mother's caregiver instead of her taking care of me, and for not having any of the fun of childhood. From that I have learned that I need to make space for the fun and joy I deserve. And I needed to grieve for my mother's and father's childhoods being filled with trauma and neglect. I'm learning that there are forces within me that are more powerful than my need to control them. I'm learning to take care of myself because the process of grieving needs to be attended to. And the deeper I go, the more I'm learning that I'm not a very good mother to myself, because I didn't have the healthy mothering I needed as a child from which to learn how to nurture myself. I need to be still and listen closely to that gentle voice within me that is usually drowned out by the noise of my ego and the world outside. I have learned that I need to give myself more love than I ever have before. And, in the deepest part of me — where I am connected to God — I know I have not lost my parents. We are eternal. This body I call Barbara will drop away. But I will still be me, and my parents are still themselves.

Children and Grieving The Loss of a Loved One

Theresa Rose, a writer and intuitive healer, recently wrote to me to share her experience of her mother's death through the eyes of Emma, her young child.

"My Mom's journey of transition into the Spirit World was just as real, powerful, painful and amazing for five-year-old Emma as it was for the rest of the family.

"Flash back to early July, just when Mom was diagnosed with cancer. My husband, Michael and I knew that we wanted to tell Emma about Mom's illness as soon as possible but had not yet figured out how to do it, as Emma's birthday was days away. We decided to wait until after her birthday to tell her. But she was already aware of the circumstances when we found her one morning lying on the living room floor. She told us about Mim (Emma's name for her Grandmother) being sick and that she already knew that she was going to go back to God. Emma was understandably sad, and my tears made her sadness even greater.

"Over the next five months, Emma and I would have countless conversations about where Mim was going when she transitioned, and Emma described Mim's next home, the Castle in the Sky. In the Castle, God welcomed everyone who died into this beautiful place filled with music, dancing, lights, and beauty. And as Emma said, 'There are fireworks of love EVERY NIGHT!' Emma's favorite drawings were of the Castle, complete with Mim, her grandma Fran (who transitioned before Emma was born), and many other angels. Emma was proud of these drawings and gave them to Mim to put by her bedside, which she often looked at.

"As Emma watched her grandma physically deteriorate, she held fast to the belief that God was taking good care of Mim, and she once said that she could see the angels that were waiting to take Mim to God. Emma discussed these things freely with her grandmother, and it was a source of great comfort to my mom knowing that Emma was leading all of us along the Spiritual path."

Months later Theresa told me that they had recently gone to see *Charlotte's Web*. When Emma watched Charlotte (a spider) die, she started to cry and continued to cry on the ride home. Theresa held her the whole time and they cried together. Theresa and Michael were glad they were able to support Emma during her outpouring of grief and continue to support her and each other in their grieving process.

Helping a Child Express Grief for Every Day Hurts, Losses or Trauma

In our psychotherapy practice, Charlie and I help adults who were repeatedly traumatized as children. We assist them in remembering the *emotional pain* connected to the trauma that they experienced. Then they can more easily and directly express and release that long held in emotional pain and the possible energy blocks associated with them.

Each buried feeling is usually magnified because these people weren't allowed to express the pain when the hurts, loss or trauma happened. So they were "re-traumatized" by not being allowed to express their hurt at the time. We hear stories of clients, as children, being threatened, shamed or warned that expressing painful feelings is not acceptable. At the severe end of dysfunctional parenting we have heard, "You've got two choices: Either I'll cut it out or you can forget about it." or "If you want to cry, I'll give you a reason to cry!" Children can also be ordered to go somewhere else until they "shape up," which just adds abandonment to their already hurting self. This denial of our children's painful feelings is what causes much disordered thinking at the least and physical or "mental illness" at the most. Recently, the Centers for Disease Control and Prevention reported that 85% of physical disease is related to emotional causes. Parents who are denying their children the ability to express their painful emotions including anger, resentment, jealousy, etc. are setting them up to become part of that 85%.

If children are allowed to express their hurt at the time it happened, then the trauma will usually dissipate. In other words, traumas don't have to be buried in our bodies and psyches, a situation that causes blocks in our energy and later can cause disease.

In the first issue of *Inspired Parenting* magazine, this quote below from Katie Gallanti, M.S. describes an important but until recently unknown dimension in healthy parenting, "Emotions can be painful and often overwhelming for young children. They need help soothing themselves when they are hurt or upset. If your child is hurt, it is a great opportunity for you to model validating his or her experience. Discouraging your little one to feel his hurt, like some well-meaning older generation parents use to do, with phrases such as 'Big boys don't cry' or 'That cannot possibly hurt that bad!' is no longer seen as a very sound child-rearing practice. In fact, this old practice is responsible for creating many an emotionally disconnected adult. Validating and comforting a child that is feeling emotionally of physically hurt is a much healthier option. If your child is hurting, comfort your child and confirm that their pain is real. Sympathy and concern are healthy responses to emotional distress in children and adults alike." (Emotional Intelligence: The Best Gift you can give your child by Katie Gallanti, M.S. *Inspired Parenting Magazine* Spring 2008 Vol 1, Issue 1)

Ethan

Here is a simple example of how a toddler can grieve if given the space.

I was babysitting for five days with my 19-month-old grandson, Ethan, while his parents took a working vacation across the country. This was the second time I was caring for him for several days. The first time he was too young to have any separation anxiety.

After dinner the first evening, he became agitated and I sat down on the floor with lots of eye contact and tried to play with him. He pushed me away and kept looking toward the front door. Then he looked into my eyes and asked me a question — half signing, half talking, half communicating heart to heart.

What I understood was, "Mommy, Daddy? Home? NOW. I want my Mommy, Mommy, Mommy. Daddy!"

He pushed me away several times when I tried to get close to him over the next one and a half hours. He chanted, "Mommy, Mommy, Mommy and Daddy" off and on.

Ethan's sobbing ebbed and flowed. Each time he pushed me away he screamed a shrill kind of "get away from me!" scream. I sank back and realized I needed to let him grieve. This little mind had figured out that his parents were not coming home that night, and he was not just fearful but angry. Finally he looked at me and I could see he was reaching from his disbelief. His mom and dad had shown up every night for his whole life of 19 months. How could they not be coming home that night?

I called the number of the hotel at about an hour into his crying. I tried to tell my daughter as unemotionally as possible what had happened. She asked if they should come home and I told her that I believed we should decide in the morning after we knew what kind of night he had. I didn't want to alarm her. But I needed to know that she might need to be prepared to leave in the morning.

About half an hour later, Ethan turned to me and in a quivering voice said, "Mommy working? Daddy working?" And I said, "Yes." And he calmed down. Four simple words. He moved into my lap and allowed me to loosely embrace him. He fell asleep in my arms.

I told Beth the next morning what had happened and we decided they should stay another day and we'd see how that night went. He cried for them for maybe 15 minutes that next evening. The next two nights were peaceful and playful at times. I had allowed him to express his grief without adding any more trauma to his experience. In return, he came back to his usual sweet and joyful self.

Every time one of our patients expresses pain over not being allowed to grieve as a child — the shaming they went through, the slaps or teasing because they were in emotional pain and needed to express it — I am grateful for letting my little grandson express his shock and pain that night. He was grieving in the most natural way, totally uninhibited.

Perhaps if all our children were allowed to express their grief spontaneously and naturally, when they grow up they wouldn't need to self-medicate with legal and illegal drugs as so many do now. And if their clinicians as children were also allowed to express their grief in this same healthy way, perhaps they would not feel the need to prescribe drugs to so many of their patients. It is possible that our "epidemic" of "depression" may be instead unexpressed grieving. Adults who were mistreated as children and not allowed to release grief become the drivers involved in road rage and even the shooters who randomly kill others and then themselves. Some have suggested (deMause 1996) that if we would raise one generation of healthy children we could go far in eradicating social violence, war and many other problems of our world.

Chapter 8

Soul Contact

Across the Veil

In the foreword of this book, Charles Whitfield writes that "...to address the Soul we have to go again beyond these three methods alone and use ontology, which is the study of being, existence, and experience. A principle way to measure these include our shared experience, whether spoken, written or expressed graphically through art. In this book, Barbara Whitfield presents numerous such shared experiences that add to our collective documentation of the existence of the Soul."

While I have already presented several such experiences, I will now, in this chapter and the next, focus on other and perhaps more compelling stories of shared experiences in which someone has died and is communicating across the veil. These experiences are more common than we may believe. Bill and Judy Guggenheim have collected 3300 accounts of cases indicative of *real* — not hallucinatory — contact with deceased loved ones, of which they have chosen to present about 10 percent, some 350 stories, in their 1995 book, *Hello from Heaven*.

Carole's Story

I had a session with Steve Rother, a well known channel a few years ago. I brought my daughter, Beth, along, and this was her first time witnessing channeling. She really didn't know what to expect but, as soon as our session was over, she got on her cell phone and told her husband, Eddie, and a few friends how amazing it was and how much she enjoyed it. To help the reader understand the story I am about to tell, I need to mention again that Beth is my only biological daughter. Kate is Charlie's biological daughter.

A few minutes into our session, Steve asked me if I had a miscarriage and was the baby a girl. He said another daughter just showed up (from the other side of the veil) and she is my daughter and the contract is still in effect. He said she is around me all the time and is actually part of my energy now. She is my guide, and this is very unusual. Usually people who have crossed over take a lot of time to acclimate before they take that position. This doesn't happen very often. I realized he was referring to Carole.

Carole came into my life here on Earth in 1996 when she was 31 years old. She was three years younger than Beth so I really was old enough to be her mother. We became instant friends. She even assisted me in creating an international conference for researchers to dialogue about "bio-energy." I in turn helped her and Rich, her husband, to create a documentary from interviews with the researchers I invited to speak.

During the four day research conference, Carole and Rich filmed 16 hours of interviews and she edited them down to a flowing 45 minutes.

I watched her take it all in and process it. I watched her dance with the concepts. I watched the concepts heal her from a short lifetime of pain and questioning. I watched her complete this lifetime without even knowing she was going to die. I watched her complete the tasks of her Soul. And then, a year later, shortly after finishing this amazing task of writing and editing she died.

As she completed the editing, she and Rich conceived their first child. And then, she miscarried the pregnancy. For the next month, she cleaned her closets out. She filled 12 large plastic bags with clothes. Her closet was practically empty. At the same time, she did the same for her relationships that were still troubling her.

During our last lunch together she told me how she had just gone to a healer who had helped her complete her unfinished business with her parents, whom she hadn't had contact with in several years. Carole told me that the healer had talked her through a guided imagery that she was hopeful about.

"I feel like I released the anger I had with my parents, especially my mother. I know this doesn't let them off the hook. They still have a lot of work to do on themselves, but I feel like I released the heaviness I was carrying.

I asked her to tell me about the guided imagery.

"The healer had me visualize each of my parents with a ball in their hands. My father's ball was green and contained my healing. My mother's was blue and contained my peace. I asked them both to throw me the balls because they belonged to me. My father threw me the ball filled with my healing, but my mother hesitated and I asked her again. Finally, she threw me the ball filled with my peace. And then I had to throw them each a ball that I could give them. I threw my father a ball filled with truth and I threw my mother a beautiful purple ball that was filled with Spirituality. The healer gave me the visual but the actual colors and meaning of each ball just appeared in my awareness. I was choked up and I know...I can feel that this was profound."

"Oh, Carole." I was feeling the fullness of her emotion now. "That's wonderful."

"Yeah! I know. My part is completed but they still have theirs. I sent him truth, and I pray he will find truth again. If my mother has Spirit helping her, I know she can reverse what they created." Carole finished in a low voice because she was choking up.

"I hope, no... I'll pray for your parents, Carole. And, Honey, I want you to know that I feel all of *our* prayers have been answered for you. You really have released... have forgiven your parents, haven't you?"

"I've thrown the ball into their court. Now it's their turn. They won't feel a tug coming from me anymore. I've let go. They need to embrace the truth now, what really happened, and then maybe they can forgive themselves," she said.

We were quiet for a long time.

※ ※ ※

What we didn't know was that Carole had been pregnant with twins. She miscarried the first but the second one lodged in the wrong place and caused her to bleed to death four days later.

Shocked and grief -stricken, Charlie and I attended her memorial service. Pictures of Carole were everywhere around us, and later I heard from several of her friends how much she loved me and how she believed I was her mother. Steve Rother was right. Carole became my daughter.

Then, finally, one day when my grieving had subsided a little, I started hearing Carole's voice in my head or I directly understood something from her in my heart. I still hear her. I hear her now helping to write this.

Kate heard Carole's voice too. Kate sings, writes songs, and plays the guitar. Right after Carole died, Kate wrote this song.

102

Our Carole's Song

I'm in the love.
I am at Peace.
Don't worry about me
'Cause now I'm free
Free to understand the answers
My life and what it means to me.

My Soul mate, my love
All we ever wanted was that
Gift from above.
I'm so sorry I had to leave
In our forever love you must believe.

You wanted to know that I'm all right
And why my body couldn't fight.
But this was all part of our plan

To help us grow, to understand.

You know I knew how peaceful life
Like this could be.
I'm with the Soul of our child
And now we both live free.

I have no fear
I am God
You I will see
Always, we will be.

The sun moon and stars
Seemed to be so far.

> Everyone already has what they're
> looking for.
> It's peace in your heart, your Soul
> Your Spirit and nothing more.
> I am like this song.
> I keep going on… And on, And on…

Rich said that the wording sounded exactly like Carole's poetry.

One evening Kate asked this voice to give her a sign that it was indeed Carole. Kate then found me in the kitchen and asked, "Can you tell me about the flowering tree on the deck?"

"Why, yes." I answered, "Carole's last birthday I took her to a garden center and told her to pick out any flowering tree she wanted for her deck. She couldn't make up her mind between two hibiscus trees so I bought both. Carole took one to her deck and I brought the other one here. To this day, I still call it 'Carole's tree.' I sit outside by it on the deck and talk to her sometimes."

Kate then told me she had asked this inner voice for a sign and it told her to ask about that flowering tree on the deck.

Witch Hazel

Kate recently reminded me of another Spiritual experience we had with Carole.

"Remember the sign from Carole after she died? It was 'Remember the witch hazel!' Do you remember that?" She asked me. "I was at work and while sitting outside under the tall trees during my lunch break, I asked for a sign and the words "remember the witch hazel" came to me. I thought, okay, this is going to sound crazy, so when I got home, you were coming down the stairs and I asked you to sit down on the couch and listen to my story. When I told you, you smiled and pointed to the bottle of witch hazel you had just set down on the table behind me as you came in and I sat down. You had been carrying it down the steps when I came in."

I did remember after all this time: 8 years. I went and looked for that bottle and found it in a bathroom closet. It was still almost full. I never use witch hazel. I probably haven't used it since that time and I don't even remember why I had it.

This is another example of communication across the veil, since this is not an ordinary coincidence. It is a meaningful coincidence, which we also call a synchroncity.

How often can a Soul move across the veil?

When I worked at the medical school at the University of Connecticut in the late 1980s, I was invited by a committee (not by the head priest) from a Catholic church to come and speak on our research into Near-Death Experiences. This took place in a small Connecticut shore town. A few weeks before the talk I was told that the head priest was against my coming and would not allow the talk to be given in the large sanctuary of the main church. The committee decided to go ahead with my talk, and hold it in the recreation building. (Back in those days this was not the first time one of my talks was "displaced.") Over one hundred people showed up for my talk and sat on folding chairs. For the first 45 minutes I described our basic research and then, as often happened, we stopped for a 20-minute coffee break. Then I continued until all the questions were answered. During the coffee break, five or six people came up to me and in low voices told me about visitations from a loved one who had died. I also heard two stories of encounters with angels. These were normal healthy people. I took a few notes and when we returned to the talk (with the permission of the tellers and without giving away their identity) I told what I had heard during the break. I then asked for a show of hands of adults who experienced some kind of visitation from "the other side," either a transitioned loved one or an angel. With a roar of laughter, almost half of the audience of over a hundred raised their hands. The question and answer period with lots of partic-ipation from the audience lasted for another hour and a half. It appeared that they too were experiencers of visitations from across the veil, and their interest and participation helped me answer some wonderful questions.

I ask this question now at other talks I give and I get about the same percentage of hands and the same roar of laughter.

A Child's Natural Ability

Theresa Rose (see page 92) wrote me the following beautiful letter about her five-year-old daughter Emma's experiences with her grand-mother, since Mim made her transition a few months ago.

"Since my mother's passing, Emma has interacted with her grandmoth-er's Spirit many times. She initially described her Mim's Spirit as a glow-ing ball of light that she saw at night when she was just about ready to sleep. After a few months, Emma expanded her visions of my mother that incorporated more detail. Emma described to me once over the breakfast table that she finds her Mim when Emma goes deep into her own heart, gets to the bottom of it, loses herself and calls God. When she does all of this, Mim makes herself known to Emma. Since Mim pro-vides Emma with a profound feeling of love, my little one frequently calls on my mother's Spirit to bring peace and joy into her life.

"Emma's Spirit language has grown beyond simply seeing the glowing ball of energy she initially saw when my mother transitioned. Through our regular discussions about Spirit and God, Emma has described feel-ing her grandmother in her heart, seeing her in the form of a bird or other animal, and hearing Mom whisper to her during quiet moments. Emma is completely comfortable with this new relationship she has with her Mim, and she calls upon her grandmother regularly for love, courage and support.

"Emma and her grandmother continue to have a very strong relationship, and the two different worlds each one occupies, the physical and the Spiritual, doesn't seem to inhibit either one of them. Emma connects to her grandmother through song, nature, mementos, and simple meditations. To her Mim is not dead; she is alive and well in the Spirit World."

Compassionate Friends

Whenever I give a talk at a support group, especially Compassionate Friends Support Groups for bereaved parents, someone will either stand during questions and answers, or will come up to me after and tell me a story of a child appearing after they have died to let the family know they are all right.

A physician and his wife told me about their child appearing at the breakfast table the morning of the child's funeral. He never said anything but there was a feeling of peace and love between them.

A young resident asked me privately if I had ever heard of another experience like his. He told me that during his first delivery as an intern, he saw a ray of light come through the ceiling and pierce the belly of the mother just before the baby's head crowned. This didn't surprise me at all because I knew of other stories in which the Soul of the baby comes and goes during pregnancy, including my own experience of Nicholas coming to me twice right after he was conceived.

Many parents told me about seeing their teenager late at night before falling asleep and then hearing their child had died in an auto accident. As painful as that sounds, it gave them a great deal of comfort to know that the child existed beyond their body.

In 1998, Carole and I did a TV show in Toronto Canada on the Near-Death Experience. This particular show had a youthful audience between the ages of 15 and 35. The producer had explained to me on the phone when he invited us that the youth of Canada were consuming a lot of anti-depressants to the point where it was reaching epidemic proportion. He hoped that a program on the Near-Death Experience would help. Before the show, Carole and I sat together in a dressing room, praying, when suddenly the host of the show burst in with the producer to tell us she had been meditating in her dressing room and when she opened her eyes, there were angels near the ceiling. She had never seen anything from the other side before and was thrilled.

When she and the producer left, Carole said, looking a little stunned, "Boy, is this going to be a show!"

And it was. Carole spoke about a profound Near-Death Experience she had when she was 17. This clip was shown at her memorial service and in her own words she told everyone there why she wasn't afraid to die.

Comas

At an IANDS support group meeting (International Association of Near-Death Studies), identical twin boys, 19-years-old, came with their mother to tell us this experience. The twins were in a bad auto accident a few months earlier. One had severe head injuries. The other was barely hurt. They both were in a coma for several days. The twin who was barely injured said he knew he had to stay with his brother on the other side because he was afraid his brother wouldn't come back. He was afraid to leave him because it was so pleasant that he might go on and not be able to return. When I asked the mother what she felt during the ordeal, she said she knew her boys well and realized that one was staying to keep the other one from going on.

When I worked at Mt. Sinai Medical Center on South Miami Beach, we had a young father in ICU in a coma from a severe heart attack. His wife tape-recorded the children at the dinner table and brought the tape in with a boom box that we placed just beyond his head, taped to the headboard. We played the tape of noise and chatter of the children 24 hours a day until he awakened. He told his wife days later that he was in the tunnel the whole time but couldn't go on because the sounds of the children's voices kept bringing him back.

And finally, there was my own father's coma. His doctor said he was in a deep coma and would die within 48 hours. Talking to him, and stroking his hair, brought him out of the coma after about a half hour. He stayed out of the coma long enough to talk to us and give us stories from his memories that we could cherish.

When he died in the middle of that night, I was sleeping on my parents' sofa in the living room. I heard someone breathing in my sleep so I opened my eyes, trying to see in the dark if it was my mother or my brother. I was alone. The breathing went on for six or more breaths and then it stopped. Within five minutes the phone rang and I knew my father had died. I wasn't with him so he came to me for his last breath.

I have experienced people coming out of comas many times just before they die. And most of them tell me about deceased relatives meeting them, either standing at the foot of their bed and communicating with no words — heart to heart — or seeing them in heavenly landscapes. Perhaps this is why I believe/know that no one dies alone. It doesn't matter if there isn't another physical being anywhere around. There are Spiritual beings greeting them with the intention of guiding them, or, as my grandmother did, letting me know she'd be there when I returned.

Chapter 9

Tom died.

Or did he?

Often referred to as the "Dean of NDE researchers," Kenneth Ring, PhD, is my friend and colleague. Ken is Emeritus Professor of Psychology at the University of Connecticut and co-founder and past president of the International Association for Near-Death Studies (IANDS). In his classic book *Heading Toward Omega* and recently in his *Lessons from the Light: What We can Learn from the Near-Death Experience*, he tells my story, including my life review. Ken also wrote extensively about Tom Sawyer (no relationship to Mark Twain's character) another Near-Death Experiencer (NDEr), who had a life review that was similar to mine in the respect that it changed him as much as it changed me and in the same ways.

I wrote Ken recently asking him for an endorsement for this book. He answered, telling me about a new article he just finished for the *Journal of Near-Death Studies* about Tom, which I will cite further below.

I met Tom at Bruce and Jenny Greyson's house when Bruce was still at the University of Michigan in the early 1980s. I drove up from where I was living in Florida and Tom drove in from up-state New York. We stayed up all that first night and talked. On the next morning, Bruce had invited three or four other NDErs from the area and anyone who wanted to come from his department. Several administrative people and a few psych residents showed up. (This meeting is depicted in my book *Full Circle*).

On that first night, Tom and I had dinner with the Greysons and then, when they went to sleep and it was just the two of us — this was the first time I was alone with another NDEr — we both opened up in a way that we NDErs crave. It's a wonderment that we share and at the same time experience a deep subtle sadness or yearning, because we sort of lost "it". It is ineffable; it can't be explained so much in words but in the looks in our eyes. It's about a feeling of love that is hard to feel here but is everywhere on the other side of the veil. Tom and I shared that. As Tom repeatedly apologized for tearing up as he told his Near-Death Experience, he told me that he was actually *reliving it* — all the overwhelming feelings that had originally marked his encounter with death. As I recounted my life review, I too could see and feel everything all over again. We both were in the same space together, even though we were in separate bodies sitting across from one another. We agreed that this was one of the big lessons of our life reviews. It's an illusion that we are separate. We really are all One! Then we told each other everything we understood in part about quantum physics explaining all this. We both were reading physics for the pure pleasure of getting closer to the Mystery. Often the tears turned into laughter as we tripped over the quantum concepts.

The meeting with the other NDErs the next day was just as "personal," with that longing for "home" hanging in the air. The others who sat behind us in an outer circle felt it. It was a powerful meeting that went on all morning.

Tom was a refreshing person. He knew he didn't have the education that put him with the "intellectuals" we were often surrounded by, but he also knew he had something to say so nothing was going to stop him. He held his own with everyone, even though his manner and choice of words were reminiscent of a character in one of Mark Twain's books. They were not as pronounced of course, but still distinct. There was a boyish charm about him that was candid and straightforward. And, if I didn't jump in that night we sat up and talked, Tom could have talked nonstop for hours!

I again visited with Tom in Connecticut at the Greysons' a few years later.

Tom Died. Or did he?

Tom died in April 2007 — too young. He had developed pulmonary fibrosis and knew he was going to die.

Carol Madec Scoville, a dear friend and associate of Tom's, shared a dream with me: "Recently, I dreamed that Tom walked up to me looking totally healthy. I said to him, 'I thought you were dead.' He laughed and said, 'Well, the nurse at hospice thought I was dead and she told everyone. Then, she came back into the room and discovered I was still alive. Believing that I would die within a couple of days anyway, the hospital staff decided not to say anything to confuse family and friends, so they didn't tell anyone. But I didn't die. I just got better and better. And here I am! I'm back!'"

Dreams like this one may be symbolic. They could also be psychic or Spiritual in a prophetic sense. The stories that follow seem to point in the same direction as Carol Madec Scoville's dream.

Ken Ring's article.

Just before I sent this manuscript to my publisher, Ken Ring emailed me about his new article that was to be published in the *Journal of Near-Death Studies* about Tom. It's called "The Death and Posthumous Life of Tom Sawyer: A Case Study of Apparent After-death Communication." After reading Ken's article, I knew I wanted to include this story of what Tom is up to now because Tom is giving us living proof that his consciousness is still alive and intact. His body may have needed to die, but Tom is experientially showing us that he is alive and well. And, he is doing this by talking to many people here — from the dimension in which he now exists. He even told Lynda, the woman you will read about below, to tell me he wants more room in this book than I think he needs! This kind of insistent sharing about the other side is just like the Tom I remember before he died.

Tom's communication with us demonstrates several cardinal character-istics of the Soul. These include: 1) The Soul is *separate from the body*, 2) The Soul *does not die*, 3) The Soul is *intelligent*, 4) The Soul is *creative*, including its ability to *extend love*, and 5) It is our *consciousness*, the intel-ligent energy in us that continues after our body and ego dies.

Tom's Life after Death

In Ken Ring's article he writes that when Tom was driven to a hospice for his final day on Earth, he chatted with one of the paramedics attend-ing him, Lynda Cummings, mentioned earlier. She had never known about life-after-death communication and she had no other contact with Tom. He died the next day. So when Tom started communicating with her a little while after his death, asking her to give his wife and sons messages, she thought she was losing her mind. Finally, after having the courage to contact Tom's wife Elaine and talk with her, Lynda was able to realize that she was not in fact losing her mind. Elaine explained to her that Tom was no ordinary man and everything Lynda was telling Elaine rang true to her because Tom manifested to her now, after death, with all of his old earthly personality quirks and mannerisms intact. He is, then, still recognizably Tom to anyone who knew him.

Tom's communication through Lynda makes perfect sense to all the others he has asked her to contact. She reports that the frequency of his presence is slowing down and that she has gotten used to it. Later, it started up again in the form of messages to me about this book.

Lynda explained that there are three ways she "hears" from Tom. First, there are detailed accounts that she wrote for Ken Ring and Sidney

Saylor Farr (the author of two books about Tom). She is usually in the middle of her everyday, crazy, busy life when Tom interrupts her. (She works as a paramedic and has 5 kids, a husband and a house to run). Each of those accounts was several pages. The second way she hears him is if she tries to focus on him while writing an email to one of his friends. She says she feels "hijacked" because he "insinuates" himself into the conversation. She explained, "I am aware of him there and what he's trying to send and I can ask, "Is that right? Is this what you meant?" When I am feeling brave I share Tom's comments and often they make sense to those who I am writing to.

The third way Lynda hears from Tom is through symbolism and synchronicities.

Lynda recently emailed a message to Tom's friends that ended: "He wants people to know he was a regular guy who had a big impact, and you can have a big impact and show others how *they* can have a big impact. Start by telling his stories where the door opens for one to be told. So don't hesitate. Even the smallest of stories can have an impact."

At the end of Ken Ring's article, Tom conveyed this thought through Lynda: "You don't just stop because you are dead; your Soul continues to love. Tom not contacting, loving and caring for his loved ones in life would be unnatural. He wouldn't ever just stop caring for loved ones. He'd never just stop. So his not contacting, touching, loving, and watching out for his loved ones NOW would also be unnatural. Some can feel it, some cannot, but he is there."

From all that I know about Tom's communications, he is telling us that *what is really important is love. All the other stuff we focus on has nothing to do with the real meaning of life: to love.*

Tom and Ken

The more I pondered Ken Ring's article, the more curious I became about Ken's involvement in all this because I know Tom loved Ken. We all love Ken, and Tom specifically told me that evening how much he loved Ken. We talked about Ken a lot because we both knew we were appearing in Ken's book *Heading Toward Omega* (Ring, 1984), and we trusted him with our deepest interpretations of what happened to us. We had to love him to trust him that much with our stories, which were so deeply personal and Spiritual. So I wrote Ken and asked if he had any contact from Tom. Ken told me he decided to keep a journal about Tom after the following encounter.

Ken received an unexpected call from his dear French friend, Andre, who informed Ken that he was in town and wanted to get together for lunch. Andre was traveling on professional business having to do with his organization, which Ken is serving on as a board member. Andre was traveling with Bob, a former board member of IANDS. Ken had originally met him a few years ago at a professional conference. Ken wrote this in his journal.

"When we met for lunch at a local café, most of our conversation, naturally, was about our board activities and related professional matters, but as we were winding down, Andre kindly asked me what was doing in my life these days. On the spur of a possibly regrettable impulse, I decided to tell him (and Bob) about my recent experiences with Tom, and what that had stirred up in me, so I first gave a brief account of Lynda's story. After that, I asked both these guys what they personally thought about this story and the possibility of life after death. And here, very unexpectedly, things turned interesting.

"When it was Bob's turn to speak, he shared that, actually, some years back he happened to find himself at a Spiritualist church in the Detroit area (where he lives). Being Jewish, he felt quite ill at ease there, but someone had told him he should develop his mediumistic gifts, and he wound up taking a ten-week course on mediumship and found that, lo and behold, he had a certain knack for it. He had some experiences during that time with discarnate Spirits that convinced him that he could at least at times have authentic contact with such beings because he was able to adduce information that turned out to be accurate, which he could not have known by normal means. Bob is a Ph.D., in some field of science, I believe (possibly physics), and he certainly doesn't practice or represent himself as a medium, but he can use these talents he's developed when he wants to.

"In any case, he told us that while we were talking about Tom, he could split his consciousness and a part of him was all this time tuning into Tom. (He later explained that when a Spirit who is still in touch with the earthly world is being talked about, it's 'as if' his line rings, as it were, and the Spirit can decide to "answer the phone." And, as it happened, Tom was "home" today and picked up. That is, joking aside, he was able to eavesdrop on our conversation and through Bob then communicate). Bob said that sometimes the information, which comes mainly through imagery, as I understood it, comes so fast that he can't grasp it all, and it's as if he has to do a kind of simultaneous translation. But the gist of what Tom communicated is that he wants it to be known that he still exists (Bob says that his personality is still intact, which fits Lynda's sense of him) and that there is life after death. This is the message he wants to communicate. Bob said that he had the sense that Tom wasn't necessarily asking me personally to be the messenger. In fact, I gather Tom doesn't care who or how many people deliver the message so long as it is conveyed. Bob also said that he picked up that Tom loved me very much and remembered fondly his days of visiting me and my family in Connecticut. (I have fond memories of those days as well). So Tom wasn't 'pushing me' specifically to do this, but I had the impression from what Bob said that Tom would be pleased if I did."

Bob also explained that in the "space" where Tom was, he seemed to be standing in a vast plain. Metaphorically speaking, if he faced the earth in an effort to communicate with human beings here, that was one thing. On the other hand, if he "turned away" to face the vast horizon, he would come into contact with much more "cosmic" things. Presumably Tom might do this some of the time, because he doesn't always seem to be "facing earth," as it were (for example, he is only intermittently present to Lynda).

Finally, Bob remarked that if Ken would like to cultivate direct contact with Tom, he could invite him into his dreams. Ken at that moment didn't believe or really know if he was all that sensitive to these realms so he just shrugged that off as believing he is too obtuse. He continues writing in his journal: "Thus far, I've had no sense of Tom after his death — I'm just too obtuse, I guess! But I suppose it wouldn't hurt to try."

And then Ken left this thought: If he was supposed to do something with all this there would be "signs" from the universe. He finished his journal entry with, "I'm still going to take a wait-and-see attitude. Not to sound grandiose or pompous, although I'm afraid this will seem both, but if 'the universe' wants me to do something, it will let me know; there will be signs."

Ken started hearing from unrelated people that Tom wanted Ken to tell his story.

Finally Lynda, in an email message, told Ken that Tom had something for him, but she didn't know what that meant. That night, Ken had this dream:

"Last night, fairly early in my sleep cycle, sometime after midnight, I awoke from a very strange experience and remember thinking, 'that's weird.' I've lost some of the details now, but as I remember, I dreamed that after having got out of my shower at home, I discovered that several things, such as stuff on my desk and computer table, had obviously been moved. But since I was alone, I could not figure out — in the dream, I mean — how this had happened. I then found myself fiddling with an old cassette player, trying to dislodge a tape of the kind I had used to record Tom — although I wasn't thinking then either of Tom or his tape. But suddenly I heard Tom's voice — distinctly — speaking to me, and as I recall, with some sense of humor. I don't recall what he was saying, but when I heard his voice, I immediately woke up with a start, which is what prompted me to say 'that's weird.'"

With that, Ken decided to write the article for *The Journal of Near-Death Studies* that is described above. In an email to Ken, Lynda expressed Tom's gratitude for starting the ball rolling and he expressed that this would lead to something else, which would then lead to something else. I believe this chapter is the first "something else," and then something else will follow from this because that's the way Tom wants it. Tom may have died, but it appears that he is still running the show!

I asked a good friend of Tom's, Kim Wise, what she thinks about all this. She calmly told me: "Sometimes I feel like he [Tom] is collaborating with me — like we are collaborators for something. He sort of moves in from the side as an impulse. And from these moments I believe he is coming in to help me or someone around me, if we are open to receiving his help. He helped us when he was alive and he is still helping us now. And if we are closed off he can't come through."

Coincidence or Synchronicity

Twenty five years ago, Tom and I sat up all night and talked about our yearning to return to that place we visited when we "died." He's there now. I am here. We are seemingly separated by a "veil" of sorts. Even though I was there for a few minutes out of linear time, I no longer yearn to be there. But I do yearn to explain "there" to us here so we can bring the realization of our Souls here. That's what this book is about — living from our Souls. We were and are our Souls when we die. That's what we yearn for now. Not a place in another dimension, but who we experienced ourselves as in that dimension. This book is an experiential description of being our Soul now. This is not only our destination, but we can live it *now* as we journey through life, as well as when we journey through death. I am grateful to Tom for continuing our conversation — 25 years later. His presence through Lynda and yes, I can feel him around me occasionally — has helped us considerably to understand what I am conveying in this book.

Some may believe that emailing Ken Ring for the first time in several months was a simple coincidence that put me in touch with Tom's new story. Ken just happened to have finished the article on Tom and asked if I'd like to read it.

I believe that Tom's story and Tom's words needed to be in this book. Something was going on to make that happen that can't be explained by our logical mind.

During the two week period of writing this chapter, the coincidences were happening fast. When a coincidence takes on special meaning for us, we call such a coincidence a synchronicity, which I address further in the next chapter.

Online Meditation

For information about meditation groups that Tom started before he transitioned, please visit my website at:

www.BarbaraWhitfield.com

Chapter 10

Cosmic Postcards:

Synchronicity and Little Miracles

Many of us didn't have a dramatic Spiritual experience that awakened us. Many awakened through the grace of synchronicities. We started to pay attention to something deeper and quieter that was sending us a wake-up call.

Synchronicities tweak us into remembering that there is more going on than our egos are willing to believe. When enough of these incidents create a thread of continuity, these meaningful "coincidences" become synchronicities. I turn on the radio and the words in the song are speaking to what I was just thinking about. I think of one of my children and the phone rings. Guess who?

I think of these as: **Cosmic Postcards**.

When I worked in research, the Near-Death Experiencers I interviewed told me about their synchronicities, and I would share some of mine with them. We ended the interviews with bright red cheeks and sparkling eyes. There's something so magical about something happening that is against all odds, all intellectual odds that is.

As I move even deeper into my authentic self, my Soul, I let these synchronicities come in and move on without telling anyone anymore because they really are hard to relay. In a momentary flash something comes in that is so meaningful to what is going on that it seems to pierce our hearts. We suddenly are paying attention to the Universe and how it weaves into our ho-hum life. I smile, say a quick "thank you" and go on.

Sometimes it's more premeditated than that. I am disturbed by something or someone's actions that I have no control over and so I pray and "turn it over" (to God). Then within a short time, a sudden opportunity opens up for me to be able to share my opinion about whatever I have no control over. This only works if I am not invested in the outcome — both the first one of having some input and then when I am given the opportunity for input, not invested in how it is incorporated.

When I am functioning as a transition team member, the synchronicities are frequent and engaging. One takes us to the next, which takes us to the next. The term "cosmic postcards" adds some humor. If this transition is a new Soul coming in — usually the humor starts with the mother in labor (between contractions). Or — at the other end of the finite half of the circle of the Soul — dying people can say some funny things. The humor feels more like someone's Soul breaking through the intensity of the moment and giving us the gift of laughter.

In Chapter Five I wrote about Sherry, a woman in her early 40s that died of cancer. Just before she slipped into a coma for her final three hours, she briefly napped and then opened her eyes and said, "I bet you thought I was dead. Well, that was just a dress rehearsal." For a few brief moments, this gathering of at least a dozen people laughed together. And, she laughed the most of all.

The Greenhouse

When I worked at the University of Connecticut in the 1980s, my two sons, Steve and Gary lived with me and attended the university there. We rented a little 650 square foot flat, one of three in this one hundred-year-old house on Main Street in Newington. The outside was covered in green aluminum siding that didn't reflect the beauty of its age. We lovingly referred to it as "Our Greenhouse," and to this day we look at pictures and tell our stories, then add, "A lot of healing went on in that greenhouse." We meant that the three of us were healing from my painful divorce from my sons' father. We healed ourselves and we healed our relationships with each other. And all three of us went to school. It didn't bother us that the plumbing in the kitchen and the bathroom was visible on the outside of the walls, as was the electrical wiring. We joked about the heavy traffic that started at 7 in the morning and continued to 11 every night. The house was so old it vibrated with every truck that went by.

Before I moved to the greenhouse, I was living in a stylish three-story town house and knew it was time to get out and find something more affordable if I was going to continue this pattern of being laid off and going to school to further my education. I asked one evening at the support group I co-led at the University for Near-Death Experiencers if anyone knew of affordable housing nearby. Sharon Grant walked up all smiles and said, "The flat above me just became available." She lived there with her preteen son. Three college students had recently moved out. My sons, Steve and Gary, and I worked hard to clean up the flat as did our two landlords. Within a month it was ready for us to move in.

The greenhouse, as Sharon showed us, was also leaning to one side. We put a can of fruit against the outer wall in the kitchen and it rolled, picking up speed on the kitchen tile, through the doorway onto the carpet. It hit the opposite outside wall with a big boom. Every time we did this, it made us laugh.

Sharon and her son, Brian, and me and my two boys became a Soul family. Gary and Steve were the brothers Brian never had. Sharon and I were Soul sisters, and we became aunts to each other's boys.

I was pink-slipped at the university for the second time because, once again, the research funding ran out. Then I was rehired a few months later. This particular story happened when I was pink-slipped for about a month and was going to school. Money was tight. My two boys and I shared the rent equally and took turns grocery shopping. I am not complaining. We learned a lot, including how to be responsible financially to ourselves and to each other, and that we could survive.

A priest called one morning and explained to me that he did a local television show. He invited me to be on it the following week and, of course, I accepted. I met him at the studio around three in the afternoon and we taped for half an hour. He told me afterwards that the tape would be shown in its entirety — no editing, which I love to hear. (I've done enough TV to know that when it is filmed and edited, we can wind up looking and sounding like idiots). And then the priest said it would be shown at midnight the next Tuesday.

I was disappointed but I didn't show it. I just left thinking, *What a waste of time! Who is ever going to stay up on a Tuesday night at midnight to watch this?*

The next Tuesday night the greenhouse was asleep, except for me as I watched and taped the half hour. The next morning I got an excited phone call from my friend, Rick Bach, who was the chairperson for Hartford AIDS Support. He told me that he spent the night with a man who died of AIDS just that morning. Around midnight they turned on the TV and there I was. He was proud to tell the man he knew me, and the two of them listened transfixed as I talked about my Near-Death Experience and what it meant to me. Rick thanked me over and over again. As we hung up, I realized that I now had the courage to call the heating oil company and ask them for an extension because it was a cold winter in Connecticut. We were going through a lot of heating oil and we couldn't meet that month's bill.

I left a message on the tape explaining. A few hours later I picked up the phone to hear the voice of the man who delivered our oil. He explained that it was his one-man company. He was excited to tell me that his brother was the priest who had interviewed me on TV. He watched the show and was so happy to hear what I said. Then he told me several times that he didn't want me to ever worry about paying my oil bill. He would never stop delivering oil to our house and it didn't matter when I paid. I could take months — or years. And then he thanked me again.

To this day, 20 years later, I still get tears in my eyes and a warm flush in my heart when I remember his phone call.

Little Miracles

A few years ago, Charlie spoke at a conference in Las Vegas at the same time Steve and Barbara Rother were having a Spiritual gathering on the other side of town. I skipped one morning's meetings and left the Las Vegas Hilton in a cab. By the time I got to this other meeting, my cab fare was extremely high. The meeting I went to that morning was all about little miracles. The premise was that we shouldn't ask God for anything specific. All we need to do is be willing and then have the awareness to see little miracles when they occur. We heard wonderful stories. When it was over the other nine people that were there exploded into what can only be described as pure joy. As we were getting ready to leave, a woman offered to drive me back to my hotel as she put her jacket on. It was a great looking satin baseball jacket and the emblem on the front said, 'Las Vegas Hilton.' "Where am I taking you?" she asked.

"To the Las Vegas Hilton!" I said laughing.

There are too many hotels to count in Las Vegas. This might not be considered a miracle, but it definitely got our attention.

Not too long ago, I was up early, around 7 am and went to my computer to check my email. I had only two new messages. I skipped the first (from a researcher at the University of Texas) and opened the one from my friend, Robynne. She wrote that she read my first draft of the chapter on Soul parenting from this book and loved it but had one sentence that bothered her. As she spelled out her objection and used her 17-year-old daughter *Frankie* as an example, I copied the few paragraphs she wrote and pasted them into the text.

Next, I opened the letter from the researcher at the University of Texas. She gave me several codes for several steps to be able to access the research over the net. My final step was my personal password, which was mine alone. It was *Frankie17.*

My heart jumped. My Soul sang. It didn't change my world. It didn't change anything. It just tugged at me in a way that little miracles do. There's no logical explanation. The odds of this happening may be a billion to one. But these little miracles only qualify as miracles because they can't be explained. There has to be something higher going on.

Twenty-four years ago (this one still gets my ego to quiet down) my first marriage of 23 years fell apart and we were in the process of working out a tough divorce. My ego was pretty sure I was going to fall flat on my face, and this assumption was being reinforced by my almost- ex-husband and our families and friends. My Soul was pleading for release. Its voice was much softer than my ego's.

I was in my car driving white-knuckled in heavy traffic with these two voices dueling in my head. "How am I ever going to get through this?" I asked as all my fear was pouring out. The truck ahead of me in stopped traffic had its license mounted so high that it was at my eye level. This Florida license plate said, "COPE." So there was the cosmic answer to my question. Not all synchronicities or cosmic postcards make our hearts fly. This one grounded me in a way that I needed. For the next several days, weeks, months and yes, years too, I saw those four important letters in front of me. I am still grateful to that truck driver for picking that word. It got me through.

I thank the Universe for all the other postcards that come to me in the way of little miracles. They feed my insatiable hunger to know. They quiet down my ego. They are my Soul's confidence because, over and over, they validate that our lives are woven and guided from something higher. This 'something higher' may be a Divine Mystery, but It shows Itself in these cosmic postcards. Even though I still have the final say on my decisions, it's so great and Soul energizing to realize that we are not alone.

Author's note: I recently wrote the foreword for Robert Perry's new book about synchronicities. Perry's book explains a detailed model for identifying meaningful coincidences and allows us for the first time to get a deeper understanding on the potential usefulness of paying attention to synchronicities. They may have more messages than we realize and this book shows how to listen in a deeper way.

Signs: A New Approach to Coincidence, Synchronicity,
Guidance, Life Purpose, and God's Plan
By Robert Perry   Semeion Press, Sedona, Arizona, 2009

Epilogue

Eternal Circle of the Soul

This book takes our happy milestones and our struggles and brings them up to the Soul level, where there is no suffering. Our false self or ego suffers by resisting, whereas our True Self and Soul look for the gift — understanding, or perhaps a lesson — and takes it in and grows more of itself. As we identify more with our Soul, it leads us to where the journey and goal are one. It was our Soul we were perhaps missing and yearning for. Our developing compassion for our self and others becomes our destination. When we meet our Real Self and our Soul, which are really one being, we are home. Here is a little story to illustrate how this all may work.

Once upon a time, a long time ago, before you and I were born, I was a little spark of light, a twinkle in God's eye. I got the news one day that I was to report again down here for another stint.

"Wait a minute. Wait a minute!" Of course 'wait a minute' was just a figure of speech because there is no time when you are a twinkle in God's eye. There is no time in eternity.

"Wait a minute," I said. "I don't want to do that again. I always wind up getting knocked around. This human business is no piece of cake, you know!"

God smiled and a tear formed in God's eye, which washed me out. I rolled down God's cheek and God caught the tear in God's hand and held it up to see me.

"You're right," God said. "It's not too good where the humans are. But we want them to remember that they are like you and me. They need to remember that they are Light and God, too. You need to go down there and help them remember."

"All right," I said, wincing. "But am I going to have to forget again who I am like I always do? Can I skip that part, please?"

"No," God said, "but I can offer you something a little different this time. You can have a peaceful life, even a happy life, as soon as you remember. It might take a while, but always choose the highest good and I'll lead you to peaceful, happy times."

How will I *know* the highest good?" I pleaded.

"Just say to yourself, 'What would God do?' And I promise you I will answer. Just listen very carefully to the softest voice within."

"What a deal," I whined. "I don't want to go back. I get so lonely."

God got another tear in God's eye because I talked about being lonely. God wiped the tear with God's other hand and we both saw another twinkle. It was you saying, "I don't want to leave God. Put me back!"

God looked at you and said, "You need to be a human again."

"Oh no," you said. "Not again. Do I have to forget who I am and all about you again? And, I get so lonely. It's not easy being human, you know. None of the others really understand yet what being human means!"

God smiled and then said to you, "Always pick the highest good and you will find yourself fast. And when you remember me, ask for this…"

And God took both hands and put them together so both tears became one. We were the brightest twinkle God had ever seen and God laughed a big laugh and said, "All right, my bright twinkles. You are going off separately now to try being human again, and when you remember to always pick the highest good, I will help you to remember your Soul and Me. And I promise you that if you do that, it will make two tears in my eyes come together and then you will find each other and be the brightest beam of Light. Oh! This is going to be Good!"

And God smiled again.

It seems like that was eons ago. But here we are, two together again. God kept God's promise. It took us a little while to figure it all out, but occasionally when you look in my eyes, there are two tears that become one because I look back into yours and I can feel God's smile in my heart."

✗ ✗ ✗

This little story has a big theme that illustrates the Soulful thoughts I am ending with: 1) If we always choose the highest good, 2) and learn to listen to the softest voice within, then, 3) we live as our natural Soul and the more Soul family we will meet.

A Wish for You

Life is miraculous

And beautiful, too.

I wish you who are reading now

This experience over and over again.

I hope you find your Soul and Its family.

I wish you peace in your hearts

and the vision that comes from seeing

through God's eyes,

The eyes of our

Sacred

Eternal

Natural

Soul.

BHW

photo by Kim Cartano

Ethan, 5, with his friend Madison.

Post-Script

Expanding Spirituality as a Genre

Harold: Maude, Do you pray?

Maude: No. I communicate.

Harold: With God?

Maude: With Life!

(from the film *Harold and Maude*, 1971)

Maude brings up an excellent point about prayer. We were taught in our traditional religions that praying is talking to or asking God. The conversation is flowing from us *to* a Supreme Being. Current writings on spirituality explain how to communicate *with* a Supreme Being/The Universe, or what we naturally perceive as something greater than ourselves — our own "God of our understanding." (Whitfield 2006).

If we pay attention to our life, as Maude suggests, we perceive an answer coming back to us. And thus, natural spirituality allows us our own interpretation. (Perry 2009).

Harvard psychiatrist George Vaillant proposes that eight positive emotions: awe, love, trust/faith, compassion, gratitude, forgiveness, joy and hope constitute what we mean by spirituality. He argues that spirituality is not about ideas, sacred texts and theology. Rather, spirituality is about emotion and social connection. His book, *Aging Well* is based on a study that prospectively charted the lives of 824 men and women for over 60 years. Dr. Vaillant concludes: "Spirituality is virtually indistinguishable from these positive emotions and is, thus, rooted in our evolutionary biology. Because these emotions are also the same ones for which most religions strive, spirituality is a common denominator for all faiths." (Vaillant 2008)

Spirituality is the *generic* umbrella term for our own intimate personal relationship with our self, others and if we choose — God. (Whitfield 2006, 2009). Individual religions are a specific *brand name*. Religion and spirituality can support one another. Some people within parts of some organized religions are afraid of the expansiveness expressed by some spiritual seekers or they confuse New Age terminology with spirituality. My colleagues and I have interviewed thousands of people who had Near-Death Experiences and we witnessed living proof that religion and spirituality can harmoniously enhance each other — or spirituality can stand alone in a well balanced peaceful life. It's our choice.

Buddhists exemplify a spiritual relationship with life almost without ever mentioning a Supreme Being (some have said that their closest word might be Shunyata, which loosely means "emptiness" or the Void). They practice compassion which extends their being to others – to all sentient beings (those who are conscious, alert, attentive, awake and responsive) and to those who still sleep or are unconscious.

Spirituality and the 'New Age" long were lumped together. I propose a separation between the two. The New Age is really old spiritual philosophy reframed so that some of us can understand it better. However, over time charlatans have moved in (as they have in other movements). They capture their audiences with charismatic personalities and aren't evolved enough to balance their ego with their new found or invented wisdom. They can sound narcissistic to many who criticize and are turned off by what they mistakenly see as "New Age." Some even teach and preach psychic abilities as the end all when that is just a development that may happen along the way. Somewhere in this confusion, people become psychic magnets for others painful emotions because no one is talking or writing about healthy boundaries. (See section on *Spiritual Bypass* in Whitfield 1995, 2006). Lately, a few of these authors and self-made gurus have turned to materialism as their agenda: how to get more, more stuff, more money, and the like.

The positive feelings, emotions and attitudes of true spirituality bring us into and beyond focusing on ourselves and into compassion for others. So we move out of the endless maze of trying to control painful, sometimes called "negative" thinking and feeling and into an openness to learning more about ourselves, others and — a Higher Power. (Whitfield 2006).

Below is a poem I wrote to help explain natural spirituality:

When the sun is hanging just below the top of the trees

And the mugginess of an August day is

Hanging on for one last hour,

I sit on our porch and wait for

The "I" in me to disappear.

My doorway to spirituality is a simple prayer,

"Here I am God with open hands."

As I look at my hands opening,

I release all the tensions and identities of the day.

Wife

Mother

Grandmother

Writer

Therapist

Senior

Wise woman —

melt into

"nobody special."

I watch giant pines, oaks and beeches

Swaying in the breeze.

I respect them for their age,

And naturally smile to them because

They are much older than me.

And, they radiate the peace

That can come with being old.

The slow fan over head gently moves away

The sticky heat and dampness

As my awareness floats into a meditation

On the swaying of the trees as they engage the wind.

These trees perform a holy dance with the spirit of the breeze.

The porch becomes a shelf for that little spark of me that is still left

And transformed into the watcher —

To witness the Universe in my piece of the world.

And to witness my peace in the world.

I melt into Spirit.

These moments bring peace and sometimes awe.

I need to become this minute so that

What little is left can dissolve into something huge —

Beyond my comprehension

Within the reach of a fleeting perception.

These moments out of time, or what we call

"The simple things" — remind me of my Spirituality.

These moments settle my mind

And bring me joy and gratitude.

BHW

Index

References

Anonymous, (1976). *A Course in Miracles*. Course in Miracles Society, Omaha, NE

Bishop, K., (2006). *The Ascension Primer: Life in the Higher Realms*. Booklocker.com, Inc.

Curtis, B. and Eldredge, J. (1997). *The Sacred Romance: Drawing closer to the heart of God*. Thomas Nelson Pub. Nashville, TN.

de Mause L. Restaging, Early traumas in war & social violence. Journal of Psychohistory 1996; 23 (4): 344-92.

Farr, S. S. (1993). *What Tom Sawyer learned from dying*. Hampton Roads, Norfolk, VA

Farr. S. S. (2000). *Tom Sawyer & the Spiritual whirlwind*. Ochamois, Berea, KY

Guggenheim B, Guggenheim J (1995). *Hello From Heaven*, Bantam, New York, NY

Inspired Parenting magazine. New Earth Publications, Inc. Hollywood, CA.

Kubler-Ross E. (1997). *On Death and Dying*. Simon & Schuster, New York, N.Y.

Moss, R. (2007). *The Three "Only" Things*. New World Library, Novato, CA.

Perry, R. (2007). *Return to the heart of God: The practical philosophy of A Course in Miracles*. West Sedona, AZ: Circle Publishing.

Perry, R. (2009). *Signs: A New Approach to Coincidence, Synchronicity, Guidance, Life Purpose, and God's Plan* Semeion Press, Sedona, Arizona.

Ring, K. (1980). *Life at Death*. Coward, McCann and Geoghegan, New York, NY

Ring, K. (1984). *Heading toward Omega*. William Morrow, New York, NY

Ring, K. and Valarino E. (1998), *Lessons from the Light*. Insight Books, New York and London

Rother, S., (2000). *Re-member: A Handbok for Human Evolution*. Lightworker.com.

Saint-Exupéry, A. (1943, 1971, 2000) A *The Little Prince* Harvest Books, Harcourt (English)

Sato, T., (2003) *The Ever-Transcending Spirit*. iUniverse, Inc. New York, NY.

Vaillant GE (2002), *Aging Well*. Little, Brown.

Vaillant GE (2008), Positive Emotions, Spirituality and the Practice of Psychiatry. In: *Medicine, Mental Health, Science, Religion, and Well-being* (AR Singh and SA Singh eds.) MSM, 6 Jan-Dec. 2008, p48-62.

Vaillant, GE (2008) *Spiritual Evolution: A Scientific Defense for Faith*. Broadway Books, New York, N.Y.

Welwood, J., "The Healing Power of Unconditional Presence." Quest 5, No. 4 (winter, 1992)

(Whitfield) Harris B & Bascom L (1990). *Full Circle: The Near-Death Experience and beyond*. Pocket Books, New York, NY

Whitfield, B., (1995). *Spiritual Awakenings: Insights of the Near-Death Experience and other doorways to our soul*. Health Communications, Inc., Deerfield Beach, FL

Whitfield, B., (1998). *Final Passage: Sharing the journey as this life ends*. Health Communications, Inc., Deerfield Beach, FL

Whitfield, B., (2009). "Mental and Emotional Health in the Kundalini Process". *Kundalini Rising: Exploring the energy of awakening*. Sounds True, Inc.

Whitfield C (1985), *Alcoholism and Spirituality*. (unpublished classic, now available from www.cbwhit.com)

Whitfield, C.L. Whitfield, B., Park, R., Prevatt, J. (2006). *The Power of Humility: Choosing peace over conflict in relationships*. Health Communications, Inc. Deerfield Beach, FL

Whitfield, C.L. (1987). *Healing the Child Within: Discovery & recovery for adult children of dysfunctional families*. Health Communications, Deerfield Beach, FL,

Whitfield, C.L. (1990). *A Gift to Myself: A personal workbook and guide to Healing the Child Within*. Health Communications, Deerfield Beach, FL

Whitfield, C.L. (1991) *Co-dependence - Healing the Human Condition. The new paradigm for helping professionals and people in recovery*. Health Communications, Deerfield Beach, FL

Whitfield, C.L. (1993). *Boundaries and Relationships: Knowing, Protecting and Enjoying the Self*. Health Communications, Deerfield Beach, FL.

Whitfield, C.L. (1995). *Memory and Abuse: Remembering and Healing the Effects of Trauma*. Health Communications, Deerfield Beach, FL

Whitfield, C.L. (2003) *The Truth about Depression: Choices for Healing*. Health Communications, Deerfield Beach, FL,

Whitfield, C.L. (2004). The Truth about Mental Illness: Choices for Healing. Health Communications, Deerfield Beach, FL

Whitfield, C.L. (2003). My Recovery: A Personal Plan for Healing. Health Communications, Deerfield Beach, FL.

About the Author

Barbara H. Whitfield, R.T., C.M.T., is the author of many published articles and four books: *Full Circle: The Near-Death Experience and Beyond*, *Spiritual Awakenings: Insights of the Near-Death Experience and Other Doorways to Our Soul*, *Final Passage: Sharing the Journey as This Life Ends*, and co-author with Charles Whitfield and Jyoti and Russell Park of *The Power of Humility: Choosing Peace over Conflict in Relationships*.

Barbara is a thanatologist, workshop presenter, Near-Death Experiencer and respiratory and massage therapist. She was on the faculty of Rutgers University's Institute for Alcohol and Drug Studies for 12 years teaching courses on the after effects of Spiritual awakenings. Barbara was research assistant to psychiatry professor Bruce Greyson, the director of research for the International Association for Near-Death Studies (I.A.N.D.S.) at the University of Connecticut Medical School, studying the Spiritual, psychological, physical and energetic after-effects of the Near-Death Experience. She is past president and a member of the board of the Kundalini Research Network and has sat on the executive board of the I.A.N.D.S. She is a consulting editor and contributor for the *Journal of Near-Death Studies*.

Barbara was a key subject in Kenneth Ring's groundbreaking book on the Near-Death Experience, *Heading Toward Omega*. He writes about her again in his latest book *Lessons From the Light*.

Barbara has been a guest on major television talk shows, including *Larry King Live*, *The Today Show*, *Man Alive*, *Donahue*, *Unsolved Mysteries*, *PM Magazine*, *Good Morning America*, *Oprah*, *Joan Rivers*, *Sonya Freeman*, and *CNN Medical News*. Her story and her research have appeared in documentaries in the US, Canada, Japan, France, Belgium and Italy and in magazines such as *Redbook*, *McCalls*, *Woman's World*, *McClean's*, *Utne Reader*, *Common Boundary*, *Psychology Today* and many others. She presented talks on the Near-Death Experience to a group in the Capital in Washington, D.C. and also the United Nations in New York.

Barbara lives in Atlanta, Georgia with her husband, author and physician Charles Whitfield, MD. They share a private practice where they provide individual and group psychotherapy for trauma survivors and people with addictions and other problems in living. For more information, go to www.barbarawhitfield.com and www.cbwhit.com.

Find More Books by Barbara Harris Whitfield

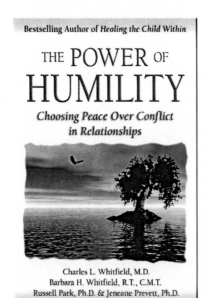

Bestselling Author of *Healing the Child Within*

THE POWER OF
HUMILITY
Choosing Peace Over Conflict in Relationships

Charles L. Whitfield, M.D.
Barbara H. Whitfield, R.T., C.M.T.
Russell Park, Ph.D. & Jeneane Prevett, Ph.D.

"This is an important book because it is about transformation of consciousness, using our relationships as our spiritual path."

Sharon K Cormier,
Registered Yoga Teacher
Near-death Experiencer

www.barbarawhitfield.com

said about the soul. In this book, we are shown the soul. Whitfield illustrated how to live from our soul and relate to the souls of others. The central concept that pervades this entire book is the differentiation between the voice and traits of the soul – who we really are – and of the ego – the character we play in our daily drama.

If the soul is who we really are, then where does the ego come from and why do we adopt it as our identity? Whitfield wrote that the soul constructs the ego as an executive assistant to help it live out this human experience: balancing the checkbook, keeping us on time for appointments, and negotiating our way through the physical world. However, when the ego takes over and controls our lives, we tend to forget who we really are. Because the ego is a construct created to negotiate our way through the physical world, it is no longer needed and dissolves when the body dies. If we make the mistake of thinking we are our egos, then we make the mistake of believing that we dissolve when we die.

Whitfield suggested a simple test to tell if you are living from your ego or from your soul, your true self: Notice what happens when you relax into "doing nothing." If you feel bored and restless, that is your ego complaining because, when you are not engaged with the physical world, it has nothing to do. On the other hand, if you have a quiet feeling of peaceful being deep within you, that is your "true self" just being. Whitfield pointed out that linear time is a construct of our intellect that moves us to living on a horizontal line. With natural spirituality, we experience time in a vertical fashion and live in the eternal now. We still meet our appointments on time, but our perception of time changes to give us a peaceful experience whereby we can focus on the task at hand and be totally present with it.

Whitfield wrote that the real love of our life is our own sacred person (of which our soul is one part), and that no other can make us whole or make us feel loved. We do that for our self in relationship with our higher power. This is "true love." In putting into words what our egos struggle to understand (but what our souls innately know), Whitfield suggested that both science and religion miss the boat in explaining what life is about. Science tries to analyze, and religion tries to codify, truths that seem so arcane to the ego, but that come naturally, requiring neither analysis nor codification, to the soul.

Whitfield punctuated her book with a series of "aha's" as she gradually learned these truths. If my experience is at all typical of other readers, we will all experience a series of "aha's" as we follow her journey through these pages. Because that journey ranges over more territory than I can cover in a short review, I'm going to focus, for illustrative purposes, on three such "aha's" that most intrigued me as a psychiatrist and near-death researcher: those related to grief, child-rearing, and death.

In discussing our tendency to live as egos rather than as souls, Whitfield tackled head-on the spiritual malaise that is endemic to our materialistic society. She pointed out that labeling our grief as "depression" can make it harder for us to move through it to resolution. We medicalize a normal human experience, numb ourselves with pills to distract our attention from our feelings, and reinforce our sense of being victims stuck in a painful situation. In grief, even though we may be overcome with sadness, we eventually move through it and make meaning out of our loss. By contrast, in depression, we are numb and do not move through the feeling. If we mislabel grief as depression and try to "treat" it with drugs, we interrupt our grief work until we stop the drugs and allow ourselves to feel the pain.

The spiritually rich growth that comes from working through grief requires us to stop trying to control the process and stop defending ourselves from our feelings. As a clinical psychiatrist, I applaud this message that the resolution lies not in denying or avoiding grief but, rather, in accepting and moving beyond it, creating a meaningful life in spite of our pain. Grief, she wrote, teaches us how to be natural and get into the flow of our inner life. It is sadly ironic that psychologists devote considerable resources to investigating the source of human happiness. As Whitfield pointed out, happiness is in fact the natural state of the soul. It is our ego that associates peace and joy with sex, drugs, and power, so that we end up wondering what it takes to satisfy us.

Turning to child-rearing, Whitfield suggested that babies are born wide awake with full contact to the divine source, but that after two or three years of confinement in physical bodies and psychological egos, they lose that sensitivity and connection, as well as the memory of who they are as souls – which she labels "soul amnesia." Whitfield described what she calls "soul parenting," a spiritual role adults can play in the lives of infants and children.

She suggested that we can influence future generations so that they will grow up in touch with their souls rather than having to seek them as adults. She pointed out that bonding doesn't necessary happen if infants have to follow what we want to do with them; it happens when we "just be" with them, play on their terms, and love them unconditionally. Likewise, sending children away to "shape up" when they act upset only adds abandonment to their already hurting self.

I found myself wondering what our world might be like if an entire generation were soul parented in the manner Whitfield outlined. Are our current epidemic of societal malaise and our addiction to prescription medications the result of our grief we were not allowed to express as children? Paradoxically, in the process of "soul parenting" the next generation, we can end up re-parenting our own souls. That is, through their eyes we get to see the world afresh and we can remember the awe of our own child-like selves. This remembrance is important because even if, as Whitfield wrote, we are here to learn to give and receive love, we cannot do so until we heal enough to be real.

Just as being with children is an opportunity to re-experience ourselves as our souls, so too being with someone who is dying provides an opportunity to help us practice being real and feeling connected. Whether we are the person dying or the person assisting in the transition, this process is a chance to put aside our egos and practice living from our souls.

Whitfield quoted from the introduction to A Course in Miracles (1975): "What is real cannot be threatened/What is unreal does not exist./Herein lies the peace of God." She wrote that if all that is real is God's world, the world of the soul, then the ego and its world are not real and, therefore, do not exist. When we make this differentiation between identifying with our true self and our false self, we learn the way to peace and serenity. However, people today have become distracted by materialism and have fallen asleep to the real world of the soul. They often wake up to their true identity and realize that they are not just their body as they about to die. At that point, they experience a sense of joy at the knowledge that the dying body is going to drop away, that suffering and death are happening to the body, not to them. When we recognize this, we can release our clinging to our false self.

Whitfield adopted Aldous Huxley's analogy from The Doors of Perception (1954) of the brain as a reducing valve, allowing the flood of too much reality to flow in a gentle stream so we can handle it without exploding. Helping someone die is usually as close as we get to the reality that is beyond our ego's ability to perceive; we do that by allowing ourselves to experience death with openness and without ego. Allowing ourselves to feel vulnerable is not bad once we recognize that we won't be destroyed, but that it is only the ego that is destroyed, while we evolve and grow. Whitfield explained that the reason people on their deathbeds see deceased relatives, and the reason she knows that no one dies alone, is that our separateness from each other is an illusion of the ego. We are our souls when we die, just as we were when we were born. To be our soul again is what we yearn for now: The divine existence we seek after death is not some place in another dimension but is who we experience ourselves as in that dimension.

Whitfield wrote that when she hears that ego voice in her head worrying that she is not qualified to help someone die, she turns the task over to the universe and asks for help to get her ego out of the way. The secret here, as elsewhere, is to relinquish control over this unpredictable process and to allow the spiritual agenda to orchestrate the transition.

The style of writing in The Natural Soul is clear and very accessible, just as it is in all of Whitfield's books. And, just as in all her previous books, this one pushes the reader a bit further than the last one did. Whitfield reminds us why NDEs are important phenomena. What I have not conveyed in this review of the major concepts in this book are the personal examples with which Whitfield illustrated these concepts. The Natural Soul overflows with intimate vignettes that bring the ideas alive.

Toward the end the book, Whitfield wrote that she has come to regard synchronicities, those meaningful coincidences that crop up in our lives, as "cosmic postcards" that remind us there is more going on than our egos are willing to believe. Her advice, when we receive one of these momentary flashes of insight into the universe, is to "smile, say a quick 'thank you' and go on." I have come to regard this book as a postcard from Whitfield's soul to ours, and my advice is to read it, say "thank you," and put it into practice.

Bruce Greyson, MD

CPSIA information can be obtained at www.ICGtesting.com
Printed in the USA
BVOW04s1657220114

342678BV00001B/369/P